SUPER
Sexy!

ANGELO COASSIN

COOK
LIKE A REAL
ITALIAN

- Super Sexy and Simple Recipes from Cooking with Bello -

PHOTOGRAPHY BY
LUKE J ALBERT

Hardie Grant

BOOKS

COOK
LIKE A REAL
ITALIAN

ANGELO
COASSIN

INTRODUCTION

Ciao! My name is Angelo (or Bello, up to you), and I am the content creator of the sexiest Italian cooking page on the internet, **@cookingwithbello**! You can find me on Instagram, TikTok, Threads, YouTube, Facebook and Pinterest.

Sometimes, I ask myself where my passion for food started, and even though I don't precisely remember, I feel like it was written in the stars. I am very Italian; I come from a beautiful region called Friuli-Venezia Giulia in the north-east of Italy, one hour away from Venice. I was born in San Daniele del Friuli, a small town famous all over the world – along with the city of Parma – for producing prosciutto crudo, a delicious cured ham. I was born on Thanksgiving, and even though we don't celebrate Thanksgiving in Italy, my aunt Maria, who lives in the US, has always called me *tacchino* (meaning 'turkey'), because I was born on 'the day of the turkey'.

If my place and date of birth are not enough to justify my passion for food, I need you to know that my family has owned a bakery for more than 150 years. In my hometown, we are known as *quelli del pane* ('those who make the bread'),

and I have always been super proud of that. After school, I used to walk to my family's bakery (it was literally a five-minute walk away) and wait until my dad was ready to go home. For me, the bakery was literally heaven. I remember entering this place full of bread, pizzas and pastries, and snacking on the most delicious food while waiting for my dad. Sometimes there was some leftover dough, and I used to play with it and make my own bread.

Growing up in an Italian household, I have always been around good food, and I remember wanting to do my homework in the kitchen while my mum and my nonna were cooking. I used to get distracted sometimes and ask them if I could help, and I'd take notes on ingredients, temperatures and cooking tips instead of doing my homework. My mum and my nonna taught me everything I know about cooking, and a lot of the recipes that I'm sharing in this cookbook come from them.

Apart from cooking, my other big passion is dancing, and I took my first ballet class when I was only three years old. I was always dancing at home as a kid, and I used to force my parents and family to watch my performances in the living room. Being a dancer in a small town was not always easy, and I used to get teased at school because of it. Fortunately, my family has always been very supportive of me and my passions, and this has encouraged me to keep dancing. Almost thirty years later, I still take my dance classes every week. Not only is it a good physical activity, but for me, it is also a spiritual practice that nourishes my soul.

I started my Instagram page during the first Covid-19 lockdown, on 26 April 2020. We all know what happened that year. All of a sudden, I found myself at home in a very tiny shared flat in central London with no job. (I had moved to London in October 2018 in order to pursue my artistic career, and until the pandemic hit, I had been performing in theatres at night and working in a café during the day.)

I am not the type of person who likes to sit around, so I decided to use this time off work to rediscover one of my biggest passions – cooking. I started to cook all the time, experimenting with new flavours and techniques, and rediscovering recipes from home that I hadn't made in a long time.

It made sense to me to share what I was doing online, and since I am not camera-shy, I decided to post my first video recipe. Slowly, people started to like what I was doing, and that encouraged me to keep sharing what I refer to now as my 'super-sexy recipes'!

A lot of people ask me why I define my food as 'super sexy', and I am always a bit confused by this question ... I mean, have you seen my recipes? I don't want to sound sassy, but how else would you describe them if not 'super sexy'? I honestly can't find a better phrase.

Another question that I get asked a lot is why I called my page 'Cooking with Bello'. Who is Bello? Well, Bello (which means 'handsome' in Italian) is a generic term that we use in Italy to refer to a friend. When I moved to the UK, all my friends used to call me Bello – and so 'Cooking with Bello' was born.

Cook Like a Real Italian is my first cookbook, and it is a collection of my favourite Italian recipes. Here, as the name suggests, you will learn how to cook like a real Italian, discovering how to make the most iconic Italian classics, such as carbonara, arancini and tiramisù, along with some modern Italian recipes that you might not be familiar with but are sure to love (see Pizza Muffins on page 17, Two-ingredient Pasta with Spinach Pesto on page 81, or my Pistachio Lava Cake on page 154).

The beauty of Italian cuisine is that not only is it the sexiest food on the planet, but all the recipes are also super easy to make. All you need are some good-quality ingredients and a little time, and you can make the most delicious meals.

I tend to simplify my recipes even more to make them as accessible as possible, so if you have never really cooked before, you can follow my recipes step by step, and I promise that you will soon be cooking like a real Italian!

INGREDIENTS

Here is a list of important information regarding some of the ingredients that you will find in this book – it's everything you need to know in order to cook like a real Italian!

PASTA

In Italy, every pasta shape has its own sauce that it's usually paired with. Depending on the shape of the pasta and the consistency of the sauce, there are some combinations that are impossible to separate and have been nonna-approved for centuries (think tagliatelle with bolognese sauce or bucatini with amatriciana sauce). In this book, you will find a lot of pasta recipes, and for each one I have suggested the perfect pasta shape. However, at the end of the day, you need to cook for yourself, so you can choose your favourite pasta shape for each recipe – just don't tell me!

FRESH BASIL

This is probably the most-used herb in Italian cuisine, and my nonna always says not to cut it with a knife, as this oxidises the leaves, making them look brown. Instead, try tearing your basil leaves with your hands.

MOZZARELLA

Most of the recipes in this cookbook require grated (shredded) mozzarella (also known as pizza mozzarella). When it comes to cooking, fresh mozzarella can be a bit tricky, as it contains a lot of water and can make your dishes soggy if it's not treated properly. You can get very good-quality grated mozzarella nowadays, and I think it's easier to use. If you want to use fresh mozzarella, however, simply drain it very well, cut it into slices and pat them dry with some paper towels. Place these slices in a sieve resting over a bowl, then cover with cling film (plastic wrap) and leave in the refrigerator overnight. During the night, the mozzarella will release most of its liquid, and will be ready to use in your recipes.

GUANCIALE

I like to call this 'Italian bacon'. It is made with pork cheek, hence the name (*guancia* means 'cheek' in Italian). Guanciale is much fatter than bacon and it has a more intense flavour. Traditionally, we use it in recipes such as carbonara and amatriciana. I know it can be difficult to source and might be a bit expensive outside of Italy, so you can easily replace it with bacon lardons or pancetta cubes instead – don't worry, my nonna will understand!

PECORINO

Pecorino is a hard, salty cheese made from sheep's milk. It has a strong flavour, which makes it perfect, again, for recipes such as carbonara and amatriciana. If you can't find it, you can simply replace it with Parmigiano (Parmesan) or Grana Padano.

Note: Unless otherwise specified, all the recipes that require an oven should be cooked in a static oven.

FREQUENTLY ASKED QUESTIONS

HOW MUCH SALT SHOULD YOU ADD TO THE WATER WHEN COOKING PASTA?

Although I've never measured out these two ingredients in my whole life (Italians are born with the knowledge of exactly know how much salt and water our pasta needs!), there is a rule. For every 100 g (3½ oz) of pasta, you need 1 litre (34 fl oz/4 cups) of water and 10 g (½ oz/ 2 teaspoons) of salt. Super easy!

DO I NEED TO BOIL LASAGNE SHEETS BEFORE USING THEM?

Let's clear this up, once and for all. No, you don't need to boil your lasagne sheets before making your lasagne. Whether you buy fresh pasta sheets or dry pasta sheets, they will both cook in the oven (just make sure you cover your lasagne sheets with a good amount of sauce and béchamel, and their liquid will help the lasagne cook to perfection). I personally prefer using fresh lasagne sheets as you can cut them and adjust them to the size of the baking dish that you are using. All the recipes in this book have been tested with fresh lasagne sheets, so if you are using dry ones, you will probably need to bake for slightly longer.

HOW DO I MAKE PIZZA SAUCE?

This is probably one of the most-asked questions on my channels, and the answer is super simple. First of all, you should never cook your pizza sauce before spreading it on your dough. That is a sin in Italy.

To make the perfect pizza sauce, simply tip some tomato passata (sieved tomatoes) into a bowl and season with salt, freshly ground black pepper and a pinch of dried oregano. Add a drizzle of extra virgin olive oil and stir to combine. Spread your pizza sauce on top of your pizza dough, or use it as a filling for calzones and *panzerotti*, and you're ready to bake!

WHAT DOES 'AL DENTE' MEAN?

Al dente literally means 'to the tooth' in Italian, and it is used to describe the perfect consistency that pasta should have after being boiled. The secret to perfect al dente pasta is to drain it 2–3 minutes before the cooking time stated on the package. At this point, you can add your al dente pasta to your sauce, along with some of the pasta cooking water, and toss everything together for a couple of minutes to combine all the flavours. Never throw away your pasta water, as it contains the super-sexy starches of your pasta, and it will make your final dish super creamy. *Mamma mia!*

WHAT DOES 'SCARPETTA' MEAN?

Scarpetta literally means 'little shoe' in Italian, and it is the action of cleaning the plate of any sauce with a piece of bread. If you make a super-sexy sauce, you don't want it to go to waste, so make sure that you learn how to do *scarpetta* like there is no tomorrow!

ANTIPASTI

ANTIPASTI

A N T I

 P

ANTIPASTI

ANTIPASTI

ASTI

ANTIPASTI

MAMMA *Mia!*

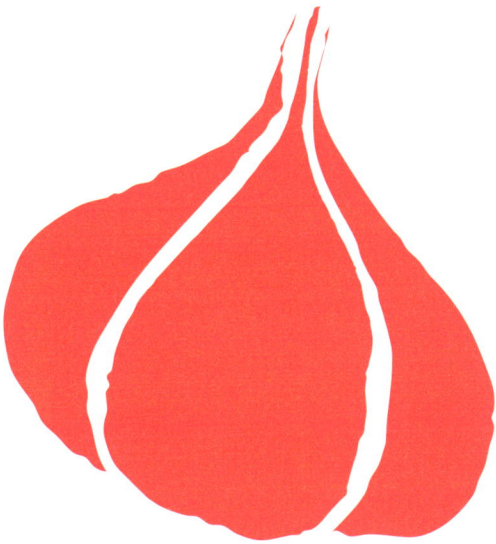

Antipasti (appetisers) are served at the start of every great Italian dinner – and, to be honest, they are my favourite part. I sometimes make entire dinners out of *antipasti*. Depending on the number of guests, I would prepare five or six of them, along with some bread and a nice charcuterie board. Open a bottle of wine, make some cocktails, and your dinner is ready!

SUPER *Sexy!*

In this chapter, you will find the recipe for my super-easy No-Knead Bread (see page 28)! You can use it to make bruschetta, or simply toast it and serve it topped with a good-quality extra virgin olive oil, some freshly ground black pepper and sea salt flakes, for the easiest – but probably sexiest – *antipasti* ever!

PARMESAN PEARLS

If you only have 10 minutes to rustle up an appetiser, I have the perfect recipe for you. These delicious Parmesan pearls are made with just two ingredients, and they are so easy to make!

100 g (3½ oz) Parmesan cheese, grated (shredded)
2 egg whites
1 litre (34 fl oz/4 cups) sunflower oil

In a bowl, combine the Parmesan and egg whites, and mix with a spoon until you have a smooth dough.

Scoop out 1½ tablespoons of this mixture and use your hands to form it into a little ball about 1 cm (½ in) in diameter.

Continue making balls until all the mixture is used up. (The recipe should make 15–20 balls.)

Pour the oil into a large, deep frying pan (skillet) over a high heat. Heat until the oil reaches 170°C (340°F). To check the oil is hot enough, simply dip the back of a wooden spoon in the oil and, if bubbles appear around it, you are ready to fry. Fry your Parmesan pearls in batches for about 6–7 minutes until … *super sexy!*

Remove from the pan with a slotted spoon and place on a plate lined with paper towels to drain, then serve with a grating of Parmesan if you like.

Buon appetito!

- Sexy Tip -

If your cheese pearls deflate when you take them out of the oil it means that they need a couple more minutes of cooking!

PIZZA MUFFINS

━━━━━━━━━━━━━━━━━━━━━━━━━━━━━━━━

- SERVES -	- PREP TIME -	- COOK TIME -
6	35 minutes, plus resting	25 minutes

These pizza muffins can be topped with your favourite ingredients – just not pineapple. *That* is NOT SEXY!

- FOR THE DOUGH -

380 g (13½ oz/3 cups) plain (all-purpose) flour
7 g (¼ oz) fast-action dried yeast
8 g (¼ oz/ 1 teaspoon) salt
240 g (8½ oz/scant 1 cup) lukewarm water

- FOR THE TOPPING -

150 g (5 oz) tomato passata (sieved tomatoes)
pinch of salt
pinch of freshly ground black pepper
pinch of dried oregano
extra virgin olive oil, for drizzling and greasing
200 g (7 oz) grated (shredded) mozzarella

In a large mixing bowl, combine the flour, yeast and salt, and mix together. Incorporate the water little by little, mixing between each addition, then continue to knead for about 4–5 minutes or until a smooth dough is formed. Cover with a clean cloth and leave to rest for 30 minutes.

In the meantime, add 100 g (3½ oz) of your tomato passata to a bowl and season it with salt, pepper, oregano and a drizzle of extra virgin olive oil.

Preheat the oven to 180°C fan (400°F) and grease a muffin tray with some extra virgin olive oil.

Using a rolling pin, roll out your dough on a clean surface to form a square about 1 cm (½ in) thick, then spread your tomato passata on top.

Roll the dough up into a sausage shape, then slice it into 12 pieces.

Place these 12 slices into the muffin tray moulds, cut sides facing up. Top with the remaining tomato passata and the mozzarella, then bake in the oven for about 20–25 minutes, or until ... *mamma mia!*

PARMESAN BISCOTTI

- SERVES -	- PREP TIME -	- COOK TIME -
4–6	15 minutes	10–12 minutes

These savoury cheese biscotti are perfect for an easy appetiser or party snack. You can make them the day before and store them in an airtight container to prevent them from drying out. Serve them alongside meats on a charcuterie board ... *mamma mia!*

125 g (4 oz/1 cup) plain (all-purpose) flour, plus extra for dusting
100 g (3½ oz) Parmesan cheese, grated (shredded)
90 g (3¼ oz) chilled unsalted butter, cubed
small bunch of thyme, finely chopped
pinch of salt
pinch of freshly ground black pepper

Preheat the oven to 180°C fan (400°F) and line a baking tray with baking parchment.

In a large bowl, combine all the ingredients and knead with your hands for a few minutes until a smooth dough forms.

On a lightly floured surface, use a rolling pin to roll out your dough to a thickness of about 4 mm (¼ in).

Cut the dough into rounds using a biscuit (cookie) cutter, re-rolling to use up the off-cuts, then place on the prepared baking tray.

Bake for 10–12 minutes, or until ... *super sexy!*

Buon appetito!

- *Sexy Tip* -

Brush your biscotti with some egg wash before baking to create a rich, golden sheen when baked.

CLASSIC & MODERN BRUSCHETTA

Bruschetta is probably one of the most famous Italian appetisers in the world, and it is honestly so simple to make, yet so delicious! Today I want to teach you all my secrets for making the perfect classic bruschetta, as well as a super-easy modern version!

- SERVES -	- PREP TIME -	- COOK TIME -
4	5 minutes, plus resting	10 minutes

- FOR THE CLASSIC -

300 g (10½ oz) cherry tomatoes, chopped
extra virgin olive oil
dried oregano, to taste
small bunch of basil
4 slices of sourdough bread
1 garlic clove
salt

Add the cherry tomatoes to a bowl and add a generous drizzle of extra virgin olive oil, along with salt and oregano to taste. Then add most of the basil and mix everything together.

Cover the bowl with cling film (plastic wrap) and allow to rest at room temperature for 30 minutes.

Drizzle some olive oil on to a griddle pan over a medium–high heat and toast your bread for 3–4 minutes before flipping over and repeating on the other side.

Cut the garlic clove in half and rub it on your toasted bread slices. Finally, pile the tomatoes and basil on top and garnish with the remaining basil and an extra drizzle of oil.

- SERVES -	- PREP TIME -	- COOK TIME -
4	5 minutes	1 hour

- FOR THE MODERN -

8 garlic cloves
extra virgin olive oil
4 slices of sourdough bread
20 cherry tomatoes, halved
2 × 150 g (5 oz) burrata
cheeses, halved
4 tablespoons pesto (see my
Classic Pesto on page 63)
salt and freshly ground
black pepper
drizzle of balsamic glaze,
to serve

To start, let's make a garlic confit. Add the garlic cloves to a small saucepan over a low heat, then pour in enough olive oil to cover them completely. Cook very slowly for about 45 minutes to 1 hour, or until the garlic is soft, buttery and creamy. Leave to cool to room temperature.

In the meantime, drizzle some olive oil on to a griddle pan over a medium–high heat and toast your bread slices for 3–4 minutes on each side.

In a small bowl, mix together the tomatoes and a drizzle of extra virgin olive oil. Season with salt and pepper and set aside.

Divide the garlic between the bread slices, spreading it out evenly, then top each slice with half a burrata. Drizzle 1 tablespoon of pesto over each, then top with the tomatoes. Serve with a drizzle of balsamic glaze on top. *Buon appetito!*

- Sexy Tip -

Always tear basil leaves with your hands for maximum flavour. Cutting them with a knife will also oxidise them, making them brown more quickly.

CHEESY POTATO FOCACCIAS

- SERVES -	- PREP TIME -	- COOK TIME -
4–6	30 minutes	10 minutes

Did you know that you can make some super-easy frying-pan focaccias with just two ingredients – potatoes and cornflour? These little focaccias are perfect for *aperitivos* and parties, and here they are filled with cheese like there is no tomorrow!

4 medium potatoes, peeled and chopped
90 g (3¼ oz/¾ cup) cornflour (cornstarch)
150 g (5 oz) grated (shredded) mozzarella
a generous drizzle of olive oil
salt

Bring a saucepan of salted water to the boil, then add the potatoes and boil for about 20 minutes, or until tender. Drain, then tip into a bowl. Mash the potatoes with a potato ricer, then add the cornflour and mix to form a dough.

Take 50 g (2 oz) of the potato dough and use your hands to flatten it into a disc about 1 cm (½ in) thick. Place 1 tablespoon of mozzarella in the centre of your potato disc, then close it on itself to form a small ball. Flatten the ball into a pancake shape. Repeat with the remaining dough and mozzarella. (The recipe should make approximately 4–6 focaccias.)

Heat the olive oil in a frying pan (skillet) over a low–medium heat for 1 minute, then cook the potato focaccias in batches for about 5 minutes on each side, or until nice and crispy on the outside. Serve straight away. *Buon appetito!*

- Sexy Tip -

Add some ham or cooked mushrooms to the cheese filling for some extra sexiness!

SCROCCHIARELLA WITH TUNA AND ONION DIP

- SERVES -
6–8

- PREP TIME -
15 minutes

- COOK TIME -
35 minutes

Scrocchiarella (meaning 'to crackle' in Italian) are super-easy homemade crackers that I like to serve as an appetiser with my delicious tuna and onion dip.

- FOR THE TUNA AND ONION DIP -

drizzle of extra virgin olive oil
300 g (10½ oz) red onions, sliced
500 ml (17 fl oz/2 cups) water
150 g (5 oz) tinned tuna
100 g (3½ oz/generous ⅓ cup) mayonnaise
½ tablespoons capers
5 anchovy fillets
1 tablespoon chopped parsley
salt

- FOR THE SCROCCHIARELLA -

50 ml (1¾ fl oz/3 tablespoons) white wine
50 ml (1¾ fl oz/ 3 tablespoons) water
100 ml (3½ fl oz/scant ½ cup) sunflower oil
1 teaspoon salt

First of all, let's prepare the tuna and onion dip. Heat a drizzle of olive oil in a saucepan over a low–medium heat. Add the sliced onions, season with salt and cook for a couple of minutes, stirring occasionally.

Add the water, ensuring the onions are completely covered. Bring to the boil and boil for 15 minutes, or until the onions are soft. Strain the onions, then tip them into a bowl and leave to cool.

Meanwhile, combine the tuna, mayonnaise, capers, anchovies and parsley in a blender. Blend until creamy. Season to taste, then stir this tuna sauce into the onions and set aside.

Now, let's make your *scrocchiarella*!

Preheat the oven to 190°C fan (400°F).

In a large mixing bowl, combine the wine, water, sunflower oil, salt, yeast and flour. Mix together with your hands for a couple of minutes, or until everything combines to form a dough.

Transfer the dough on to a clean surface and continue to knead for a few more minutes.

2 teaspoons fast-action
dried yeast
290g (10¼ oz/2⅓ cups) plain
(all-purpose) flour
small bunch of rosemary, leaves
picked and roughly chopped
sea salt flakes

Place the dough on top of a sheet of baking parchment, then use a rolling pin to roll it out into a thin rectangle of about 40 × 25 cm (16 × 10 in). Transfer the dough to a baking tray, then sprinkle over some salt flakes and fresh rosemary.

Bake for 15 minutes.

Allow your *scrocchiarella* to cool on the tray, then use your hands to break it into big pieces. Place them on a serving dish and serve with the tuna and onion dip. *Buon appetito!*

PANCETTA-WRAPPED PRAWNS

- SERVES -	- PREP TIME -	- COOK TIME -
6	15 minutes	15 minutes

My mum made these prawns for the first time as an appetiser on Christmas Day a few years ago, and they were a huge success. Serve them with a glass of Aperol spritz to make a super-sexy *aperitivo*.

20 king prawns (shrimp)
20 thin pancetta or bacon slices
160 g (5½ oz) ready-rolled puff pastry
1 egg
2 tablespoons sesame seeds

Preheat the oven to 180°C fan (400°F) and line a 30 × 18 cm (12 × 7 in) baking tray with baking parchment.

Prepare the prawns by removing the heads and shells. Keep the tails and remove the intestinal threads with a toothpick. Wash the prawns under cold water, then dry with a paper towel.

Wrap each prawn in a slice of pancetta or bacon.

Slice the puff pastry into 20 strips (each about 3 cm/1¼ in wide), then wrap a pastry strip around each pancetta-wrapped prawn.

In a bowl, beat the egg, then brush it on to each prawn.

Place the wrapped prawns on the prepared baking tray and sprinkle the sesame seeds over the top.

Cook for 10–15 minutes until nice and golden, then serve. *Buon appetito!*

- Sexy Tip -

Try wrapping your prawns (shrimp) with some *lardo di Colonnata*, a typical Italian lard, for some extra sexiness.

EASY NO-KNEAD BREAD

- SERVES -
6–8

- PREP TIME -
10 minutes, plus resting

- COOK TIME -
40 minutes

I'll be honest with you: in my family, we are not allowed to make bread or buy it at the supermarket. My uncles own a bakery in my hometown, and that's the only bread allowed in my house. However, the bakery closes for a couple of weeks each summer, and during that time, Dad makes his own bread at home (of course he is not going to cheat on his family by buying the bread in another bakery!). This is the recipe he uses. If you have never made bread before, you have to try this! It is so easy to make, and you don't need any special equipment or skills.

500 g (1 lb 2 oz/ 4 cups) bread flour, plus extra for dusting

7 g (¼ oz) fast-action dried yeast

9 g (¼ oz/ 1 teaspoon) salt

320 ml (11¼ fl oz/ 1⅓ cups) lukewarm water (about 50°C/ 120°F)

In a large bowl, combine the flour, yeast and salt and mix together. Add the water, a little at a time, stirring with a wooden spoon between each addition until it's well combined. Cover with cling film (plastic wrap) and leave to rest at room temperature for 2½ hours.

Transfer the dough to a floured surface and sprinkle some extra flour on top. Use your hands to fold the dough over itself at least 15 times, then shape it into an oval.

Cover the dough with a clean dish towel or a piece of cling film, and leave to rest for another 20 minutes.

Meanwhile, place a casserole dish (Dutch oven) with its lid in a cold oven, then preheat the oven to 230°C fan (475°F).

Once the oven reaches temperature, remove the hot casserole dish with the help of some oven gloves, then carefully place a sheet of baking parchment at the bottom of the dish. Transfer the dough to the hot casserole dish, then cover with the hot lid and return to the oven to bake for 30 minutes.

After this time, carefully remove the lid, then bake the bread uncovered for another 10 minutes. Allow to cool a bit before serving it. *Buon appetito*!

– Sexy Tip –

If you don't own a casserole dish, you can use an oven–safe glass dish with a lid or a cake tin (pan) with some foil on top.

VEGGIE AND RICOTTA SQUARES

- SERVES -
4

- PREP TIME -
10 minutes

- COOK TIME -
55 minutes

I always make these ricotta squares for picnics or as a quick lunch at the beach. They are honestly super easy to make, and they are delicious either warm or cold. Did I mention that they are completely gluten-free as well?

180 g (6½ oz) carrots, diced
180 g (6½ oz) peas
500 g (1 lb 2 oz) ricotta
3 eggs
40 g (1½ oz) Parmesan cheese, grated (shredded)
120 g (4 oz) plain yoghurt
60 g (2 oz/ ½ cup) potato starch
10g (½ oz/ 2 teaspoons) salt

Preheat the oven to 160°C fan (350°F) and line an 18 cm (7 in) square baking dish with baking parchment.

Bring a saucepan of water to the boil. Add the carrots and cook for 5 minutes, then add the peas and cook for another 5 minutes. Drain and set aside.

In a large bowl, combine the ricotta, eggs, grated cheese, yoghurt, potato starch and salt, and mix together with a hand mixer for a minute or until smooth.

Stir in the peas and carrots, then pour your mixture into the prepared baking dish.

Bake for 40–45 minutes, then let the mixture cool a little bit before cutting it into nine squares. Serve – *buon appetito!*

- Sexy Tip -

You can replace the peas or carrots with ham or salami.

FRIED GNOCCO

- SERVES -
6–8

- PREP TIME -
1 hour 30 minutes

- COOK TIME -
10 minutes

Gnocco fritto (or *torta fritta*) is a classic Italian fried dough, typical of the Emilia–Romagna region. It is perfect as an appetiser, served with a nice platter of ham, salami and cheeses instead of the usual slices of bread or crackers. Don't forget a glass of red wine to make everything ... *super sexy*. *Buon appetito!*

160 ml (5½ fl oz/ scant ¾ cup) milk
1 teaspoon dried brewer's yeast
350 g (12 oz/ generous 2¾ cups) plain (all-purpose) flour, plus extra for dusting
30g (1 oz) lard, at room temperature
pinch of salt
1 litre (34 fl oz/ 4 cups) olive or sunflower oil, for deep-frying

Pour the milk into a mug or jug and heat in the microwave for 30 seconds or until lukewarm. Pour it in a large bowl with the yeast. Stir to combine and leave to rest for 10 minutes.

After 10 minutes, add the flour, lard and salt to the bowl and mix everything together with a fork until a dough forms. Transfer the dough to a clean surface, dust with flour and knead for 10 minutes using the palms of your hands.

If the dough looks too dry in the beginning, don't worry – that's completely normal. Keep kneading and your dough will soon become ... *super sexy!*

Form the dough into a ball and place it back in the bowl. Cover with a clean dish towel and leave to rest for 1 hour at room temperature.

Lightly flour your work surface, then roll out your dough with a rolling pin until you have a sheet about 5 mm (¼ in) thick. Using a sharp knife or pastry cutter, cut the dough into 5 cm (2 in) squares.

Pour the oil into a large, deep frying pan (skillet) over a high heat. Heat until the oil reaches 170°C (340°F). To check the oil is hot enough, simply dip the back of a wooden spoon in the oil and, if bubbles appear around it, you are ready to fry. Fry your dough pieces in batches for about 1 minute on each side, or until they become puffy and golden.

Remove from the pan with a slotted spoon and place on a plate lined with paper towels to drain. Serve warm with some Parma ham or salami. *Buon appetito!*

– Sexy Tip –

For a vegetarian alternative, you can substitute the lard with the same quantity of extra virgin olive oil.

CRISPY POTATO CAKE

- SERVES -
4–6

- PREP TIME -
10 minutes

- COOK TIME -
1 hour–1 hour 30 minutes

This super-easy potato cake (*tortel di patate* in Italian) is a typical appetiser from the Trentino-Alto Adige region in the north of Italy. You can serve it with ham, salami or a nice cheeseboard, and it is perfect for a winter *aperitivo*!

50 g (2 oz) unsalted butter
1.6 kg (3 lb 8 oz) potatoes, peeled and grated (shredded)
80 ml (2¾ fl oz/ ⅓ cup) water
80 ml (2¾ fl oz/ ⅓ cup) milk
salt and freshly ground black pepper

Preheat the oven to 200°C fan (425°F) and grease a 35 × 25 cm (14 × 10 in) baking tray with the butter.

In a large bowl, mix the grated potatoes with the water and milk. Season with salt and pepper, then transfer the potato mixture to the prepared baking tray. Bake your potato cake at the very bottom of your oven (yes, the tray should literally be at the bottom of the oven) for about 1 hour to 1 hour and 20 minutes, or until a nice golden crust forms at the bottom – you can check by lifting up a corner. Check on it from time to time to make sure it is not burning.

Move the potato cake from the bottom of the oven to under the grill at the top of the oven. Cook for a further 5–10 minutes to make the top nice and golden.

Cut into squares and serve with cheeses, salami and ham. *Buon appetito!*

FOOLPROOF FOCACCIA

- SERVES -
6

- PREP TIME -
10 minutes, plus resting

- COOK TIME -
40 minutes

Focaccia is probably the most famous Italian bread in the world, and we have so many different types! In the Liguria region, they make their focaccia super soft and with a lot of extra virgin olive oil, or extremely thin and filled with cheese; in the city of Bari, they add boiled potatoes to the dough and top their focaccia with olives and tomatoes. Here, I want to share my family recipe: which is similar to Liguria's bread and perfect enjoyed plain, for making sandwiches, or served with some salami and ham on a charcuterie board.

500 g (1 lb 2 oz/ 4 cups) bread flour
7 g (¼ oz) fast-action dried yeast
400 ml (14 fl oz/ generous 1½ cups) lukewarm water
2 tablespoons extra virgin olive oil, plus extra for greasing
9 g (¼ oz/ 1 teaspoon) fine salt

- FOR THE TOPPING -

3 tablespoons extra virgin olive oil
salt flakes, to taste
small bunch of rosemary, leaves picked

In a large bowl, mix together the flour and yeast. Add the lukewarm water, a little at a time, mixing between each addition, then knead the mixture for a couple of minutes, or until the water has been completely absorbed. Now add the olive oil and salt, and keep kneading for about 3–4 minutes, or until you have an elastic dough.

Cover the bowl with cling film (plastic wrap) and leave your dough to rest in a warm place for a couple of hours.

Preheat the oven to 190°C fan (400°F) and grease a 28 × 21 cm (11 × 8 in) baking tray with 2 tablespoons olive oil.

After 2 hours, transfer the dough to the prepared tray. Cover the tray with cling film and let the focaccia rise for another 20 minutes.

Grease your fingers with some olive oil, then use them to make the classic deep dimples in the focaccia dough. Allow the dough to rest for a further 10 minutes.

Meanwhile, for the topping, drizzle the olive oil over the dough, then sprinkle over the salt flakes and rosemary leaves.

Bake for about 40 minutes, or until nice and golden. Then cool for 20 minutes before serving.

Buon appetito!

- Sexy Tip -

Top your focaccia with some sliced onions before baking for extra sexiness!

PRIMI

PRIMI

P

PRIMI

PRIMI

R I M I

PRIMI

MAMMA *Mia!*

SUPER *Sexy!*

If you like carbs, this is going to be your favourite chapter! *Primi* (the first course) is definitely the central – and maybe the most important – part of a classic Italian meal. These recipes are the ones that have made Italian food famous all over the world, and you will find some delicious new surprises as well!

This chapter features some iconic Italian sauces, such as pesto, bolognese and marinara, which you can use in different and maybe unexpected ways. These sauces are, of course, wonderful with pasta, but try drizzling some pesto on a bruschetta or over a salad, or using marinara as a dip for your pizza crusts ... *mamma mia!*

CLASSIC CARBONARA

- SERVES -	- PREP TIME -	- COOK TIME -
4	10 minutes	15 minutes

Carbonara is definitely one of the sexiest dishes in Italian cuisine. It is super easy to make – and no, you *don't* need cream! Did you know that it was invented by a chef from Rome as an homage to the American soldiers who liberated Italy during World War Two?

5 egg yolks
50 g (2 oz) Pecorino cheese, grated (shredded)
150 g (5 oz) guanciale, trimmed and chopped into
1 cm (½ in) lardons
400 g (14 oz) spaghetti
salt and freshly ground black pepper

– Sexy Tip –

If you can't find guanciale, you can replace it with pancetta or bacon. And if you can't find Pecorino cheese, you can replace it with Parmigiano or Grana Padano; it's not the original recipe, but it's still ... *super sexy!*

In a bowl, mix the egg yolks with the grated cheese until you have a smooth paste. Set aside.

In a frying pan (skillet) over a medium heat, sizzle your guanciale lardons for about 8–10 minutes, or until nice and crispy. Remove from the pan and set aside on a plate, but don't clean the pan.

Bring a large saucepan of salted water to the boil over a medium heat. Add the spaghetti and cook for 2–3 minutes less than indicated on the packaging until al dente. Drain, reserving a couple of ladlefuls of the pasta water, then add the spaghetti to the pan you used to fry the lardons.

Place over a medium heat and toss for 90 seconds to combine all the flavours, adding half a ladleful of the reserved pasta water.

Turn off the heat, then add the cheese and egg yolk mixture. Stir vigorously with a wooden spoon until you have a creamy sauce, adding some more of the reserved pasta water if necessary.

Finally, add your crispy guanciale lardons, give it one last stir, then serve with a sprinkling of ground pepper and cheese on top. *Buon appetito!*

SUMMER LASAGNE

This no-pasta lasagne is so easy to make; it's the perfect idea for a quick summer dinner! You can be creative with the filling and use any leftovers you have in the refrigerator. Try adding some ham between the layers or stirring some spinach into the ricotta cream to make your lasagne ... *super sexy!*

2 large courgettes (zucchini)
500 g (1 lb 2 oz) ricotta
150 g (5 oz) pesto (see my Classic Pesto on page 63)
120 g (4 oz) Parmesan cheese, grated (shredded)
200 g (7 oz) grated (shredded) mozzarella
drizzle of extra virgin olive oil
salt and freshly ground black pepper

- Sexy Tip -

Because we are using raw courgettes, your lasagne might release some excess moisture while baking, but don't worry! Carefully tilt the dish and remove excess liquid with a spoon.

Preheat the oven to 180°C fan (400°F) and line a 24 × 12 cm (9½ × 4½ in) baking dish with baking parchment.

Trim the ends of your courgettes, then, with the help of a potato peeler, slice them lengthways into very thin slices, about 1 mm thick.

Arrange the courgette slices on a flat plate, layer with paper towels and repeat until all the slices are used up to remove any excess moisture. Set aside.

In a food processor, combine the ricotta and pesto with 100 g (3½ oz) of the grated Parmesan. Season with a pinch of salt and pepper and blitz for about 30 seconds until creamy.

Arrange one layer of your courgette slices in the prepared baking dish, then cover with 3 tablespoons of the ricotta and pesto mixture. Sprinkle 2 tablespoons of the grated mozzarella on top, then repeat this layering process until all your ingredients are used up.

On top of the last layer, sprinkle any remaining cheese.

Bake for about 35 minutes, or until ... *super sexy!* Remove from the oven and let your lasagne rest for 5 minutes before serving.

PENNE ALLA VODKA

- SERVES -	- PREP TIME -	- COOK TIME -
4	5 minutes	20 minutes

Penne alla vodka is a classic Italian pasta recipe from the 1980s, and it is super easy to make. Traditionally, this sauce is served with penne, but rigatoni and spaghetti will also work perfectly.

drizzle of extra virgin olive oil
1 onion, finely chopped
1 red chilli, finely chopped
1 bay leaf
50 ml (1¾ fl oz/ 3½ tablespoons) vodka
300 ml (10 fl oz/ 1¼ cups) tomato passata (sieved tomatoes)
80 ml (2¾ fl oz/ ⅓ cup) double (heavy) cream
360 g (12½ oz) penne pasta
salt and freshly ground black pepper
small bunch of parsley, finely chopped, to serve

Heat the olive oil in a frying pan (skillet) over a low–medium heat. Add the onion, chilli and bay leaf, and sizzle for a couple of minutes. Add the vodka and let it completely evaporate (this will take a couple of minutes), then add the tomato passata. Season with salt and pepper and cook for 15 minutes, stirring occasionally.

Finally, add the cream and cook for a further 5 minutes.

Meanwhile, bring a large saucepan of salted water to the boil over a medium heat. Add the pasta and cook for 2–3 minutes less than indicated on the packaging until al dente. Drain, reserving a couple of ladlefuls of the pasta water.

Add the pasta to your sauce and toss well over the heat to combine all the flavours, adding a drop of pasta water to loosen if necessary. Serve topped with parsley. *Buon appetito*!

- Sexy Tip -

Add some smoked pancetta and chopped garlic to your sauce for some extra flavour!

CREAMY MUSHROOM RISOTTO

- SERVES -
4

- PREP TIME -
30 minutes

- COOK TIME -
1 hour

Risotto is a dish typical of Italian cuisine. Make sure you use the right type of rice to make your risotto; arborio and carnaroli are best, as they contain more starches than other varieties and will make your dish super creamy!

drizzle of olive oil
250 g (9 oz) mushrooms
2 garlic cloves
320 g (11¼ oz/ scant 1½ cups) risotto rice (carnaroli or arborio)
60 ml (2 fl oz/ ¼ cup) white wine
15 g (½ oz) unsalted butter
50 g (2 oz) Parmesan cheese, grated (shredded)
small bunch of parsley, chopped

- FOR THE VEGETABLE STOCK -

1.5 litres (51 fl oz/ 6 cups) cold water
1 celery stalk
1 carrot, peeled
1 onion, peeled
1 tomato
small bunch of parsley
salt and freshly ground black pepper

First, let's prepare your vegetable stock. Pour the water into a large pot, then add the celery, carrot, onion, tomato and parsley. Season with salt to taste, then bring to the boil and cook for 30 minutes. Strain through a sieve, then pour the strained stock back into the pot and keep it hot.

To make the risotto, heat the olive oil in a 25 cm (10 in) frying pan (skillet) over a medium heat. Thinly slice the mushrooms and add them and the garlic to the pan, and cook for 10 minutes, stirring occasionally. Stir in the rice and toast it for a couple of minutes, or until translucent.

Add the white wine and stir for 4–5 minutes until the liquid is absorbed. Add a couple of ladlefuls of the hot vegetable stock and stir everything together, making sure that the stock fully covers the rice.

Keep stirring and continue adding more stock every time the liquid is absorbed. This will take about 16–18 minutes.

Turn off the heat, remove the garlic cloves and add the butter, Parmesan and most of the parsley. Stir one last time, then sprinkle the remaining parsley on top. *Buon appetito!*

CLASSIC BOLOGNESE SAUCE

- SERVES -	- PREP TIME -	- COOK TIME -
4–6	12 minutes	2+ hours

This is probably the most famous Italian sauce on earth, and it is super easy to make. The secret is to let your sauce simmer very slowly for at least 1–1½ hours. The more time you give it, the better your sauce will be (in Naples, they simmer it for 24 hours – just saying). The resulting bolognese should not be very liquid, but should instead be a thick and meaty sauce where the meat has absorbed most of the tomatoes' juices.

drizzle of extra virgin olive oil
1 onion, finely chopped
1 celery stalk, finely chopped
1 carrot, finely chopped
100 g (3½ oz) pancetta rashers
(or thin bacon), finely chopped
250 g (9 oz) minced
(ground) pork
350 g (12 oz) minced
(ground) beef
50 ml (1¾ fl oz/ 3 tablespoons)
red wine
100 ml (3½ fl oz/ ½ cup) milk
400 g (14 oz) tomato passata
(sieved tomatoes)
2 tablespoons tomato
purée (paste)
salt and freshly ground
black pepper

Heat the oil in a large saucepan over a low–medium heat. Add the chopped onion, celery and carrot. Cover with a lid and cook for about 8–10 minutes, stirring occasionally.

Add the pancetta and cook for 5 minutes more, or until the pancetta becomes translucent. Now add the minced pork and beef and cook for another 5 minutes or until browned, breaking it up with your spoon. Stir in the wine, then, when it has completely evaporated (which will take 3–4 minutes), pour in the milk as well. Simmer for another 10 minutes.

Season with salt and pepper, and finally add the tomato passata and tomato purée. Cover with a lid and reduce the heat to low, then leave your bolognese sauce to simmer for at least 1½ hours, stirring occasionally.

Your classic bolognese sauce is now ready. You can use it to make a lasagne, or serve it with some pasta or gnocchi. *Buon appetito!*

MY DAD'S BOLOGNESE LASAGNE

- SERVES -	- PREP TIME -	- COOK TIME -
4–6	20 minutes	55 minutes

My dad is the king of lasagne in my family, and today I want to share his famous recipe with you. To make life easier, I suggest you use fresh pasta sheets for this, as you do not need to boil them first (you can find them in most supermarkets nowadays).

300 g (10½ oz) fresh lasagne sheets
1 quantity Classic Bolognese (page 51)
200 g (7 oz) Parmesan cheese, grated (shredded)

- FOR THE BÉCHAMEL SAUCE -
(MAKES 500 ML/ 17 FL OZ/ 2 CUPS)

50 g (2 oz) unsalted butter
50 g (2 oz/ scant ½ cup) plain (all-purpose) flour
500 ml (17 fl oz/ 2 cups) milk
pinch of ground nutmeg
salt

Preheat the oven to 170°C fan (375°F).

First of all, let's make the béchamel sauce. Melt the butter in a saucepan over a low–medium heat, then add the flour a little at a time, mixing between each addition with a wooden spoon until a paste is formed. Now, slowly incorporate the milk, adding it a little at a time and stirring well between each addition – I suggest using a whisk to prevent any lumps from forming. Whisk continuously for 8–10 minutes, or until you have a thick sauce. Stir in the nutmeg and season with salt.

Spread some béchamel sauce across the bottom of a 30 × 40 cm (12 × 16 in) oven dish, then add a layer of fresh lasagne sheets. Top with 4 tablespoons of the bolognese sauce, followed by some grated Parmesan cheese, and cover with some more béchamel. Repeat these layers until all the ingredients are used up, and don't forget to add a generous amount of grated Parmesan cheese on top – this will form a nice crust once it is baked.

Cover with foil and bake for about 40 minutes, then remove the foil and bake, uncovered, for a further 5 minutes to make your lasagne … *super sexy!*

Remove the lasagne from the oven and allow it to rest for 5 minutes before serving. *Buon appetito!*

PASTINA

- SERVES -
4

- PREP TIME -
5 minutes

- COOK TIME -
25 minutes

I like to call this dish 'Italian penicillin', because it's what Italian parents give to their kids when they're sick! The name of this dish comes from the name of the pasta shape that we use, pastina, which literally means 'small pasta'. If you can't find it, don't worry; orzo will work just as well (I actually prefer it). Serve this for dinner on a cold, rainy day to immediately feel better!

500 g (1 lb 2 oz) chicken stock
300 g (10½ oz) orzo or pastina pasta
70 g (2¼ oz) unsalted butter
1 egg
80 g (3 oz) Parmesan cheese, grated (shredded)
freshly ground black pepper

Pour the chicken stock into a saucepan over a low–medium heat and bring to the boil. Once boiling, add the orzo or pastina and cook for the time indicated on the package (it usually takes 10–15 minutes), or until the stock has reduced and the pasta is fully cooked.

Turn off the heat, then add the butter and egg and stir vigorously for 90 seconds, or until the butter has melted and the egg is fully incorporated. Finally, add the grated Parmesan and stir once again.

Serve with some black pepper on top (I don't add salt to this recipe, as both the stock and the cheese are very salty already, but you can add a little to taste if you want). *Buon appetito!*

- Sexy Tip -

Place your butter in the freezer for about 10 minutes before adding it to the pastina. The thermal shock between the super-cold butter and the very hot pastina will make your dish super creamy ... *mamma mia!*

PASTA PASTICCIATA

- SERVES -	- PREP TIME -	- COOK TIME -
4	15 minutes	50 minutes

This oven-baked pasta will win your heart; it's cheesy, full of flavour and super easy to make, perfect for a quick Sunday lunch! Here, I'm giving you my mum's recipe, but you can take this as inspiration and modify it to use up any leftover ingredients that you have in your refrigerator!

drizzle of olive oil
1 small onion, finely chopped
2 Italian sausages, skins removed, chopped
500 g (1 lb 2 oz) tomato passata (sieved tomatoes)
250 g (9 oz) Béchamel Sauce (see page 52; halve ingredients)
350 g (12 oz) rigatoni pasta
200 g (7 oz) grated (shredded) mozzarella
60 g (2 oz) Parmesan cheese, grated (shredded)
salt

– Sexy Tip –

If you don't have time to make your own béchamel sauce, you can buy it at the supermarket; it is often sold as 'white sauce' or 'lasagne sauce'.

Preheat the oven to 180°C fan (400°F).

Heat the olive oil in a frying pan (skillet) over a low–medium heat. Add the onion and sausages and cook for 3–4 minutes, or until the sausage meat turns brown. Add the tomato passata, then season with salt and cook for 15 minutes, stirring occasionally. Next, stir in the béchamel sauce.

Meanwhile, bring a large saucepan of salted water to the boil over a medium heat. Add the pasta and cook for 2–3 minutes less than indicated on the packaging until al dente. Drain, then stir it into your sauce, along with 150 g (5 oz) of the mozzarella and half of the Parmesan.

Transfer your pasta to a baking dish and top with the remaining mozzarella and Parmesan. Cover with foil and bake for 25–30 minutes, removing the foil for the last 5 minutes so you get a nice golden crust on top. *Buon appetito!*

FRESH RED WINE TAGLIATELLE

- SERVES -	- PREP TIME -	- COOK TIME -
4	20 minutes, plus resting	2 minutes

Perhaps you've made fresh pasta before, but have you ever made it with red wine? This is my Aunt Gabriella's super-easy fresh pasta recipe! Serve it with some bolognese ragù (see page 51) or a creamy cheese sauce to make it ... *mamma mia!*

400 g (14 oz/ 3¼ cups) durum wheat flour (often called '00' flour, pasta flour or semolina flour), plus extra for dusting
200 ml (7 fl oz/ scant 1 cup) red wine
salt

- Sexy Tip -

You can use your favourite red wine for this recipe, but I would suggest using a Brunello di Montalcino or Lambrusco. Also, do not use plain (all-purpose) flour for this recipe, as it will completely change the consistency of your pasta.

Add the flour and red wine to a food processor and blitz for about 30 seconds or until it comes together to form a dough.

Transfer the dough to a clean surface and knead for about 5–6 minutes until smooth. You should have a fairly hard dough that is quite difficult to knead. Cover the dough with cling film (plastic wrap) and leave to rest at room temperature for 30 minutes.

After 30 minutes, cut the dough in half and roll out each half on a lightly floured surface until about 1 mm thick. While you work with the first half of the dough, cover the other half with some cling film to prevent it from drying out. If your dough is not stretching enough, let it rest for a couple more minutes to allow it to relax and you'll be able to roll it out more easily.

Finally, slice your pasta sheets into 5 mm (¼ in) strips. And there you have it, your own homemade red wine fresh tagliatelle.

To cook, bring a large saucepan of salted water to the boil over a medium heat. Add the tagliatelle and cook for about 2 minutes, then serve with your favourite sauce. *Buon appetito!*

HOMEMADE MARINARA

- SERVES -	- PREP TIME -	- COOK TIME -
4–6	10 minutes	35 minutes

Marinara is the most versatile of Italian sauces. You can use it as the base for other recipes, as a sauce for pasta and pizza, or even as dip. Stop buying it at the supermarket, and instead make your own marinara at home. It is super easy and it tastes *much* better!

drizzle of olive oil
1 onion, diced
4 garlic cloves, finely chopped
100 ml (3½ fl oz/ scant ½ cup) white wine
2 × 400 g (14 oz) tins peeled tomatoes
handful of parsley, chopped
handful of basil, chopped
salt and freshly ground black pepper

Heat the oil in a sauté pan over a low–medium heat. Add the onion and sizzle for about 3 minutes, then add the garlic and cook for 30 seconds more. Pour in the white wine and cook for a few minutes more until the alcohol has evaporated completely.

Add the tomatoes, crushing them with the spoon as you stir them in. Season with salt and pepper to taste, then add the parsley and half of the basil. Cover with a lid and leave to simmer for about 30 minutes, stirring occasionally.

After 30 minutes, add the remaining basil and stir once more. If you like, you can blend your sauce for 30 seconds at this stage to make it even smoother.

Your homemade marinara sauce is now ready. *Buon appetito!*

- Sexy Tip -

You can use your favourite white wine for this recipe. My absolute favourite is Ribolla Gialla, but Pinot Grigio or Vermentino will work well too.

CLASSIC PESTO

- SERVES -
4

- PREP TIME -
8–10 minutes

Genoese pesto is considered the king of Italian condiments. Traditionally, it has been used to garnish pasta and gnocchi, and nowadays we also use it on pizza, in salads and even on meat. I want to show you how to make this pesto using a traditional marble mortar, but if you don't own one, you can simply add all the ingredients to a food processor and whizz everything together for 35–40 seconds or until creamy.

80 g (3 oz) basil leaves
2 garlic cloves
35 g (1¼ oz) pine nuts
3 g (1/8 oz/ ½ teaspoon) salt
40 g (1½ oz) Pecorino cheese, grated (shredded)
40 g (1½ oz) Parmesan cheese, grated (shredded)
70 g (2¼ oz) extra virgin olive oil

Wash the basil leaves under cold running water, then gently pat them dry with a clean dish towel.

Add the garlic cloves to a marble mortar. Work the garlic with a wooden pestle until it becomes a cream.

Add the pine nuts and continue to work with the pestle. When you have a smooth paste, add the basil leaves and salt. Start by crushing the leaves with the pestle, then begin making rotary movements, being careful to incorporate any pieces that remain at the edges.

When you once again have a creamy consistency, add the Pecorino and finally the Parmesan. Continue working the pestle until all the ingredients come together and look creamy. At this point, you can add the oil, little by little, mixing well with the pestle. Once it is all incorporated, your pesto is ready. *Buon appetito!*

- Sexy Tip -

If you make your pesto with a food processor, add an ice cube before mixing to make your pesto vibrantly green!

RICOTTA GNOCCHI

- SERVES -	- PREP TIME -	- COOK TIME -
4	15 minutes	3–4 minutes

If you like classic Italian gnocchi, you have to try this super-easy version using ricotta instead of potatoes! I love to make these gnocchi and I usually serve them with melted butter, fresh sage and grated cheese. They also pair perfectly with a simple tomato sauce, a cheese sauce, or some basil pesto.

500 g (1 lb 2 oz) ricotta
1 egg
50 g (2 oz) Parmesan cheese, grated (shredded)
pinch of ground nutmeg
300 g (10½ oz/ scant 2½ cups) plain (all-purpose) flour, plus extra for dusting
salt

In a mixing bowl, combine the ricotta, egg, grated cheese and nutmeg. Season with a pinch of salt and mix with a whisk for 1 minute. Incorporate the flour, adding it a little at a time, and then knead everything for about 2–3 minutes, or until all the ingredients come together to form a smooth dough.

Divide the dough into four and roll each piece into a sausage shape about 2 cm (¾ in) in diameter. Cut this into 1.5 cm (⅝ in) pieces and place on a lightly floured surface or plate. Cover with a clean cloth to prevent them from drying out while you make the rest of the gnocchi.

Bring a saucepan of salted water to the boil over a medium heat. Working in batches to avoid overcrowding the pan, boil your ricotta gnocchi for 3–4 minutes until they float to the surface, then remove with a slotted spoon and serve with your chosen accompaniments. *Buon appetito!*

- Sexy Tip -

Make sure you do not overknead your dough, as it will make your gnocchi super hard, which is NOT sexy!

PASTA ROSES

- SERVES -	- PREP TIME -	- COOK TIME -
4	20 minutes	45 minutes

If you have some fresh lasagne sheets at home and you want to find a different way of using them, you have to make these super-easy pasta roses! This is a traditional dish of the Emilia-Romagna region, and it is the perfect idea for a dinner with your family and friends.

250 g (9 oz) fresh
lasagne sheets
500 ml (17 fl oz/ 2 cups)
Béchamel Sauce (see page 52)
120 g (4 oz) Parmesan cheese,
grated (shredded)
350 g (12 oz) Provolone cheese
400 g (14 oz) sliced ham

Preheat the oven to 180°C fan (400°F).

Arrange your fresh lasagne sheets on a clean surface. Spread a couple of spoonfuls of béchamel sauce on top of each lasagne sheet, then sprinkle over a tablespoon of grated Parmesan. Top with each one with a slice of Provolone cheese and a slice of ham. Roll up each lasagne sheet, then cut each roll into thirds.

Spread some béchamel sauce across the bottom of an oven dish, then arrange your lasagne rolls, cut side up, on top. Top with the rest of the béchamel sauce and scatter over the remaining Parmesan. Cover with foil and bake for 40–45 minutes, removing the foil for the last 5 minutes so the top becomes nice and crispy. *Buon appetito!*

- *Sexy Tip* -

If you want to use dried lasagne sheets instead, simply boil them in some salted water for a few minutes less than the time indicated on the package (it's best for them to be very al dente, as they will keep cooking in the oven), then drain and let them cool on a clean dish towel before proceeding with the recipe.

CLASSIC AMATRICIANA

- SERVES -
4

- PREP TIME -
10 minutes

- COOK TIME -
40 minutes

I have to admit it, amatriciana is probably my favourite pasta dish ever. I like to think of it as the older sister of carbonara, with similar flavours and just as much sexiness! Pair it with a nice glass of red wine to be transported immediately to Rome.

150 g (5 oz) guanciale, trimmed and chopped into 1 cm (½ in) lardons
50 ml (1¾ fl oz/3 tablespoons) white wine
500 g (1 lb 2 oz) tomato passata (sieved tomatoes)
1 small red chilli, chopped
400 g (14 oz) bucatini pasta
100 g (3½ oz) Pecorino cheese, grated (shredded)
salt and freshly ground black pepper

In a frying pan (skillet) over a medium heat, sizzle your guanciale lardons for 8–10 minutes or until nice and crispy. Add the white wine and let it evaporate for 3–4 minutes, then remove your crispy guanciale from the pan (keeping the pan on the heat) and set aside on a plate.

Add the tomato passata and chilli to the now-empty pan. Season with salt and pepper, reduce the heat to low–medium, and cook for 20 minutes, stirring occasionally. After 20 minutes, add the crispy guanciale back into the pan.

Bring a large saucepan of salted water to the boil over a medium heat. Add the bucatini and cook for 2–3 minutes less than indicated on the packaging until al dente. Drain, reserving a couple of ladlefuls of the pasta water.

Add the drained bucatini to your sauce. Toss well for a couple of minutes to combine all the flavours, adding a drop of pasta water if necessary.

Turn off the heat, add the cheese and give it a nice stir, then serve. *Buon appetito!*

SPAGHETTI FRITTATA

- SERVES -	- PREP TIME -	- COOK TIME -
6	10 minutes	30 minutes

This traditional Neapolitan recipe was originally created to use up leftover pasta, and it's the perfect way to use up any leftover ingredients you have in the refrigerator. This is my personal take on it. Make it for picnics or bring it with you for a super-sexy lunchbreak in the office. You can eat it cold or simply reheat it in the microwave!

400 g (14 oz) spaghetti
olive oil, for drizzling
250 g (9 oz) smoked
pancetta cubes
6 medium eggs
100 g (3½ oz) Parmesan cheese,
grated (shredded)
150 g (5 oz) smoked
Provolone cheese, diced
100 g (3½ oz) grated
(shredded) mozzarella
salt and freshly ground
black pepper

Bring a large saucepan of salted water to the boil over a medium heat. Add the spaghetti and cook for 2–3 minutes less than indicated on the packaging until al dente. Drain, then tip into a bowl with a drizzle of olive oil so the spaghetti strands don't stick together.

Meanwhile, fry your pancetta cubes in a 25 cm (10 in) non-stick frying pan (skillet) over a medium heat for about 6–7 minutes or until golden, then set aside.

Beat the eggs in a bowl, then add the Parmesan, Provolone and mozzarella cheeses, along with the fried pancetta. Season with black pepper, then add the drained spaghetti and mix all the ingredients together.

Over a medium heat, add a generous drizzle of olive oil in the same pan you used to cook your pancetta in, then add the spaghetti mixture. Flatten your pasta with the back of a spoon so it covers the base of the pan, then cover with a lid and cook for about 6–7 minutes, or until the eggs have set and you have a golden crust at the bottom of your frittata.

Now it's time to cook the other side of the frittata. Use a large round plate with a larger circumference than that of the pan. Set it on top of the pan, then, with a quick but careful movement, flip the plate and the pan together so the frittata ends up on the plate.

Slide it back into the pan to cook on the other side for another 4–5 minutes, or until … super sexy!

Arrange the spaghetti frittata on a large serving plate and cut into slices. *Buon appetito!*

SPINACH AND RICOTTA CRESPELLE

- SERVES -	- PREP TIME -	- COOK TIME -
4–6	15 minutes	1 hour

Crespelle are the Italian savoury version of French crêpes. They are usually filled with vegetables and covered with a lot of white sauce and cheese. Along with lasagne and pasta bakes, *crespelle* are a classic Sunday dish. You can prepare them the day before, store them in the refrigerator and bake them when you're ready.

2 eggs
125 g (4 oz/ 1 cup) plain (all-purpose) flour
300 ml (10 fl oz/ 1¼ cups) milk
drizzle of extra virgin olive oil

- FOR THE FILLING -

drizzle of extra virgin olive oil
600 g (1 lb 5 oz) fresh spinach
150 g (5 oz) ricotta
80 g (3 oz) Parmesan cheese, grated (shredded)
500 ml (17 fl oz/ 2 cups) Béchamel Sauce (see page 52)
salt

To make the *crespelle*, crack the eggs into a bowl, then add the flour and milk. Whisk to combine and create a creamy mixture.

Heat the olive oil in a small (16 cm/ 6¼ in) non-stick frying pan (skillet) over a low–medium heat. Pour a ladle of the *crespelle* mixture into the pan, tilting it to make sure the base is fully covered. Cook for 2–3 minutes, or until the edges become slightly brown. Flip the *crespella* with a spatula and cook on the other side for 1 minute. Transfer to a plate, then repeat with the remaining mixture until it is all used up.

Preheat the oven to 180°C fan (400°F).

To make the filling, heat a drizzle of extra virgin olive oil in a large frying pan over a low–medium heat. Add the spinach and season with a pinch of salt, then cook for 10 minutes. Set aside to cool.

In a large bowl, combine the ricotta with 60 g (2 oz) of the Parmesan and your cooled, cooked spinach. Stir everything with a fork to combine.

Take your first *crespella* and spoon some of the spinach and ricotta mixture on to one half, then fold the other half over the top and close the edges carefully, ensuring the filling doesn't come out. Repeat to fill the rest.

Spoon 4 tablespoons of the béchamel sauce into a 20 × 30 cm (8 × 12 in) oven dish and spread out to cover the base. Add the stuffed *crespelle*, then pour in the remaining béchamel sauce and sprinkle over the rest of the Parmesan.

Bake for 10 minutes, or until the *crespelle* have a light brown colour on top. *Buon appetito!*

- Sexy Tip -

You can stuff your *crespelle* with your favourite ingredients. Try ricotta and smoked salmon, or mushrooms and Scamorza cheese … *mamma mia!*

PASTA ALLA ZOZZONA

- SERVES -	- PREP TIME -	- COOK TIME -
4	10 minutes	30 minutes

Pasta alla zozzona literally means 'dirty pasta' and it is a typical Roman dish. I prefer to call it 'happy pasta', because it is so creamy and rich that I always make it when I need something to cheer me up.

drizzle of olive oil
250 g (9 oz) Italian sausage, skins removed, chopped
150 g (5 oz) guanciale, trimmed and chopped into 1 cm (½ in) lardons
400 g (14 oz) cherry tomatoes, halved
5 egg yolks
50 g (2 oz) Parmesan cheese, grated (shredded), plus extra to serve
360 g (12½ oz) rigatoni pasta
salt

Heat the olive oil in a frying pan (skillet) over a low–medium heat. Add the sausage and guanciale and cook for about 15 minutes until browned, stirring occasionally. Add the tomatoes to the pan, then cover with a lid and cook for a further 10 minutes, stirring occasionally.

Meanwhile, combine the egg yolks and grated cheese in a small bowl and mix with a fork to create a cream.

While the sausage mixture is cooking, bring a large saucepan of salted water to the boil over a medium heat. Add the pasta and cook for 2–3 minutes less than indicated on the packaging until al dente. Drain, reserving a couple of ladlefuls of the pasta water.

Tip the pasta into the pan with the sausage mixture. Toss well for 90 seconds to combine all the ingredients. Turn off the heat, then add the cheese and egg mixture and stir vigorously until completely incorporated, adding a drop of pasta water to loosen if necessary.

Serve topped with more grated Parmesan. *Buon appetito!*

- Sexy Tip -

If you can't find guanciale, you can use bacon instead.

ROASTED TOMATO SOUP

- SERVES -	- PREP TIME -	- COOK TIME -
4–6	10 minutes	50 minutes

This classic Italian soup is perfect for cold winter days. I like to serve it with a drizzle of mozzarella cream on top to make it ... *mamma mia!*

1 kg (2 lb 4 oz) tomatoes, halved
1 large onion, peeled and halved
1 garlic bulb, halved through the middle
drizzle of extra virgin olive oil
small bunch of basil
250 ml (8½ fl oz/ 1 cup) water
100 ml (3½ fl oz/ scant ½ cup) single (light) cream
salt and freshly ground black pepper

- FOR THE MOZZARELLA CREAM -

200 g (7 oz) mozzarella
30 ml (2 tablespoons) single cream

- Sexy Tip -

Try making this soup with red peppers instead of tomatoes, and burrata instead of mozzarella for the cream.

Preheat the oven to 200°C fan (425°F) and line a baking tray with baking parchment.

Arrange the tomatoes, onion and garlic on the prepared tray and drizzle generously with olive oil. Season with salt and pepper, then roast your veggies for 40–45 minutes.

Remove from the oven and tip the roasted tomatoes and onion halves into a blender. Squeeze the garlic cloves out of their skins and add them to the blender too, along with the basil. Whizz everything together until smooth.

Transfer this mixture to a large saucepan over a low–medium heat. Add the water and single cream, and season with salt to taste. Bring to a simmer and let your soup bubble for a couple of minutes.

Meanwhile, prepare the mozzarella cream. Add the mozzarella and single cream to a clean blender and season with a pinch of salt. Blend everything together for 1 minute.

Serve the roasted tomato soup with a drizzle of mozzarella cream on top and a slice of toasted bread on the side. *Buon appetito!*

CHEESY POTATO RAVIOLI

- SERVES -
4

- PREP TIME -
30 minutes

- COOK TIME -
40 minutes

These super-easy potato ravioli are a staple recipe in my family. We often make them for special occasions, but they are so easy to make that sometimes we also have them for lunch during the week too. The dough is the same as a classic potato gnocchi dough, so you can also use this recipe to make traditional gnocchi.

150 g (5 oz) Gorgonzola cheese
150 g (5 oz) Parma
ham, chopped
80 g (3 oz) unsalted butter
salt and freshly ground
black pepper
50 g (2 oz) Parmesan cheese,
grated (shredded), to serve

- FOR THE DOUGH -

1 kg (2 lb 4 oz) potatoes, peeled
and chopped into large pieces
300 g (10½ oz/ scant 2½ cups)
plain (all-purpose) flour, plus
extra for dusting
1 medium egg

Begin by making the dough. Bring a large pan of salted water to the boil, then add the potatoes and boil for 20–25 minutes until tender. Drain and tip into a large bowl, then mash using a potato ricer. Leave to cool completely.

Once cool, add the flour and egg to the potatoes. Season with a pinch of salt and knead for about 3–4 minutes, or until all the ingredients come together to form a smooth dough.

Using a rolling pin, roll out your dough on a floured surface to a thickness of 5 mm (¼ in), adding a little more flour if necessary.

Using a glass or a round pastry cutter with a diameter of about 6 cm (2½ in), cut out approximately 30 circles from the dough, re-rolling the dough to use up off-cuts.

Fill each circle with ½ teaspoon of Gorgonzola cheese, then fold into a half-moon shape, gently pressing down the edges with your fingers or the tines of a fork so your ravioli won't open while cooking.

– Sexy Tip –

When making the dough, it is very important that you let your potatoes cool completely before adding the flour. If they are still warm, they will require more flour, which will make your dough super hard when it comes to boiling your ravioli. Another secret is to never overknead your potato dough; just knead it until all the ingredients come together.

Bring a large pan of salted water to the boil and cook the ravioli for 4–5 minutes until they float to the surface, then drain.

Meanwhile, cook the Parma ham in a large frying pan (skillet) over a medium heat for about 5 minutes or until crispy. Transfer to a plate, then add the butter to the now-empty frying pan. Melt the butter and season with black pepper, then add your drained ravioli and toss well for a minute to coat.

Serve topped with Parmesan cheese and the crispy Parma ham. *Buon appetito!*

TWO-INGREDIENT PASTA WITH SPINACH PESTO

- SERVES -
2

- PREP TIME -
10 minutes

- COOK TIME -
5 minutes

If you only have 15 minutes to make dinner, you have to try my super-easy two-ingredient spinach pasta recipe. It will honestly change your life, and all you need is flour, spinach, a food processor and some scissors! If you have kids, this is a great way to hide some extra veggies in their food.

- FOR THE DOUGH -

150 g (5 oz/ scant 1¼ cups)
all-purpose (plain) flour
130 g (4½ oz) fresh spinach

- FOR THE SPINACH PESTO -

30 g (1 oz/ scant ¼ cup)
cashews
1 garlic clove
50 g (2 oz) Parmesan cheese
150 g (5 oz) fresh spinach
50 g (2 oz) basil leaves
50 ml (1¾ fl oz/ 3 tablespoons)
extra virgin olive oil
pinch of salt

To make the pasta dough, add the flour and spinach to a food processor. Blitz for 35–40 seconds, or until a dough forms. It's fine if the dough is a bit sticky – don't add extra flour, otherwise your fresh pasta will become hard once it's cooked. Flatten your dough into a disc about 4 cm (1½ in) thick.

Bring a large pan of salted water to the boil. Hold your dough disc over the pan of boiling water and use some kitchen scissors to cut off 3 cm (1¼ in) chunks, letting them fall into the water. Cook for 4–5 minutes, or until the pieces float to the surface. Drain, reserving some of the cooking water.

Meanwhile, to make the pesto, add all the ingredients to a blender and season with salt to taste. Blitz for 30–40 seconds until smooth, then transfer the sauce to a large bowl.

Add the drained pasta to the bowl and stir to coat it in the sauce, adding a drop of pasta water if necessary. Serve topped with some extra grated Parmesan. *Buon appetito!*

BAKED RICOTTA BALLS

- SERVES -	- PREP TIME -	- COOK TIME -
6	20 minutes	50 minutes

My mum used to make these super-cheesy baked ricotta balls for Sunday lunch when I was a kid, and they are so easy to make! You can use your favourite vegetables for the filling. Here, I've used spinach, but squash and courgettes (zucchini) will work perfectly as well!

20 g (¾ oz) unsalted butter
50 g (2 oz/ scant ⅔ cup) breadcrumbs, plus 2 tablespoons for the baking dish
drizzle of extra virgin olive oil
800 g (1 lb 12 oz) fresh spinach
500 g (1 lb 2 oz) ricotta
2 eggs
40 g (1½ oz) Parmesan cheese, grated (shredded), plus 3 tablespoons for the topping
a pinch of ground nutmeg
100 g (3½ oz/ generous ¾ cup) plain (all-purpose) flour
250 g (9 oz) Provolone cheese, sliced
500 ml (17 fl oz/ 2 cups) Béchamel Sauce (see page 52)
salt and freshly ground black pepper

Preheat the oven to 180°C fan (400°F). Grease a 20 × 30 cm (8 × 12 in) baking dish with the butter and then scatter the 2 tablespoons breadcrumbs all over. Set aside.

Heat the olive oil in a large frying pan (skillet) over a low-medium heat. Add the spinach and season with a pinch of salt, then cook for 10 minutes until wilted. Allow to cool completely before chopping.

Tip the ricotta into a bowl and break it up with a fork. Add the chopped spinach, along with the eggs, the 40 g (1½ oz) Parmesan, and the nutmeg. Season with salt and pepper and stir well to combine. Now add the 50 g (2 oz/⅔ cup) breadcrumbs and mix again.

Shape the mixture into small balls of about 40 g (1½ oz) each (you should get about 30). Tip the flour into a shallow bowl and dip the ricotta balls into the flour to coat. Place them in the prepared baking dish.

Arrange the Provolone cheese slices on top, then pour over the béchamel sauce. Scatter the remaining 3 tablespoons of Parmesan on top, then cover with foil and bake in the oven for 40 minutes, removing the foil for the final 10 minutes of cooking time so a nice crust can form on top. Serve and enjoy.

LEMON PESTO LINGUINE

- SERVES -	- PREP TIME -	- COOK TIME -
4	10 minutes, plus soaking	10 minutes

I had lemon pesto for the first time five years ago, during a holiday on the Amalfi Coast. I immediately fell in love with it. It is perfect served with pasta for a quick summer lunch, and you can also spread it on toasted bread and top with some burrata to make a delicious bruschetta.

50 g (2 oz/ ⅓ cup) cashews
zest of 1 lemon and juice of 2
small bunch of parsley
6 basil leaves
1 garlic clove
40 g (1½ oz) Parmesan cheese,
grated (shredded)
80 ml (2¾ fl oz/ ⅓ cup) extra
virgin olive oil
360 g (12½ oz) linguine
salt and freshly ground
black pepper

– Sexy Tip –

For some super-sexy alternatives, try mixing your pasta and lemon pesto with some good-quality tinned tuna, or serving your lemon pesto linguine with some burrata on top.

Put the cashews into a bowl and pour over enough room-temperature water to cover. Leave to soak for 1 hour, then drain.

Tip the drained cashews into a blender, along with the lemon zest and juice, parsley, basil, garlic, Parmesan and olive oil. Season with salt and pepper, then blitz everything together until creamy.

Bring a large saucepan of salted water to the boil over a medium heat. Add the linguine and cook according to the instructions on the packaging. Drain, reserving a couple of ladlefuls of the pasta water.

In a large bowl, combine the linguine with your lemon pesto, tossing to coat and adding a drop of pasta water if necessary. *Buon appetito!*

SECONDI

SECONDI

SECONDI

SECONDI

S E C

O N D I

SECONDI

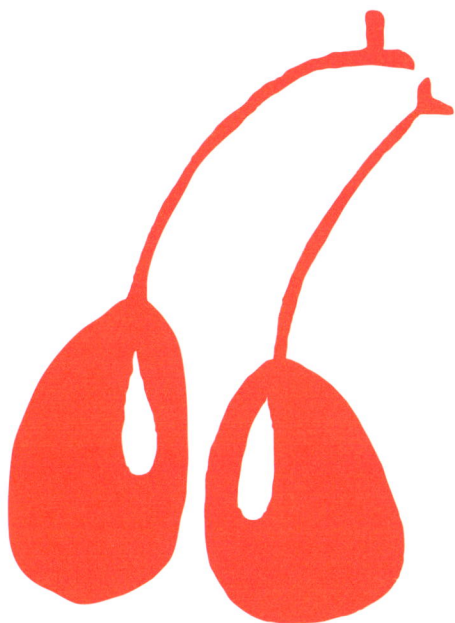

Italian food is not all about pasta, and, in this chapter, you will probably discover some recipes that you didn't even know existed. *Secondi* (the second course) usually consists of meat, fish and vegetable dishes that we serve as the main meal. In this chapter, I have also included my super-easy homemade pizza; it is honestly the easiest recipe ever, and you don't need any baking skills to make it!

MAMMA *Mia!*

Some of these recipes are dishes that I grew up with and hold dear in my heart, so I am super happy to share them with you all!

What I love about this chapter is that it literally covers recipes from the whole of Italy: you will find recipes from the north (*Frico* on page 98), the centre (Bolognese *Cotolette* on page 105), and the deep south (Sicilian Cod on page 115). Get ready to travel around Italy in just a few pages!

CHEESY LEMON SCALOPPINE

- SERVES -	- PREP TIME -	- COOK TIME -
4	10 minutes	15 minutes

I always make these super-cheesy lemon *scaloppine* when I want something delicious for dinner but I don't have a lot of time to cook. If you want to make them extra sexy, try replacing the lemon juice with Marsala wine!

2 skinless and boneless chicken breasts
50 g (2 oz/ scant ½ cup) plain (all-purpose) flour
50 g (2 oz) unsalted butter
50 ml (1¾ fl oz/ 3 tablespoons) lemon juice
50 g (2 oz) Provolone cheese, sliced (or use mozzarella)
salt and freshly ground black pepper

Cut each chicken breast in half horizontally so you end up with four chicken steaks. Place each steak into a Ziplock bag and pound it with a rolling pin until it is about 6 mm (¼ in) thick. Gently dust each steak with flour and set aside.

Melt the butter in a frying pan (skillet) over a medium heat. After a couple of minutes, when the pan is hot and the butter is sizzling, add your chicken steaks and cook for a couple of minutes on each side.

Reduce the heat to low–medium, pour the lemon juice over the chicken and season with salt and pepper, then cook for a further 5 minutes on each side or until the chicken is cooked through. (Always make sure that your chicken is fully cooked before consuming it, and remember that the cooking time may vary depending on the thickness of your chicken steaks.)

Turn off the heat and place the cheese slices on top of your *scaloppine*. Cover the pan with a lid and let the cheese melt in the residual heat for a couple of minutes until ... *super sexy!* Serve with a sprinkle of pepper and lemon slices if you like.

- *Sexy Tip* -

Serve your lemon *scaloppine* topped with some fresh rocket (arugula) and cherry tomatoes.

PIZZA IN TEGLIA

- SERVES -	- PREP TIME -	- COOK TIME -
4–6	10 minutes, plus resting	30 minutes

If you have never made pizza before, you have to try this super-easy recipe! I call it 'fool-proof pizza'. You don't need any special equipment, and you will probably already have all the ingredients in your cupboards and refrigerator at home. In Italy, this is exactly the type of pizza that you would find in bakeries, and it is the perfect thing to rustle up for a dinner with your friends! Here, I have given the instructions for a classic margherita pizza, but you can choose your own favourite toppings. Be creative (but not *too* creative – pineapple on pizza is absolutely *not* accepted!).

- FOR THE DOUGH -

500 g (1 lb 2 oz/ 4 cups) plain (all-purpose) flour

7 g (¼ oz) fast-action dried yeast

10 g (½ oz/ 2 teaspoons) caster (superfine) sugar

400 ml (14 fl oz/ generous 1½ cups) lukewarm water

50 ml (1¾ fl oz/ 3 tablespoons) extra virgin olive oil, plus extra for greasing

10 g (½ oz/ 2 teaspoons) salt

To make the dough, combine the flour, yeast and sugar in a large bowl and give it a stir. Add half of the water and half of the olive oil, and stir again until all the ingredients are incorporated. Add the salt, followed by the remaining water and olive oil. Mix for a couple of minutes until you have a smooth and super-sticky dough.

Cover the bowl with some cling film (plastic wrap) and leave to rest in a warm place for a couple of hours or until the dough has doubled in size.

Preheat the oven to 200°C fan (425°F).

Brush a generous amount of olive oil over a 30 × 40 cm (12 × 16 in) baking tray. Place your sticky pizza dough on top and gently spread it out with your hands to cover the tray.

- FOR THE SAUCE -

400 g (14 oz) tomato passata
(sieved tomatoes)
dried oregano, to taste
drizzle of extra virgin olive oil
salt and freshly ground
black pepper

- FOR THE TOPPING -

300 g (10½ oz) grated
(shredded) mozzarella
small bunch of basil,
leaves picked

To make the sauce, combine the tomato passata, oregano and olive oil in a small bowl. Season with salt and pepper and mix to combine, then pour it on top of your dough. Spread it out evenly with the help of a spoon, then leave your pizza to rest for 10 minutes.

Bake the pizza for about 25 minutes, then remove it from the oven, scatter over the mozzarella, and bake for a further 5 minutes. Garnish your pizza with some fresh basil leaves and serve. *Buon appetito!*

STUFFED COURGETTES

- SERVES -	- PREP TIME -	- COOK TIME -
4	15 minutes	1 hour

My Aunt Maria makes the best stuffed courgettes (zucchini) in the whole world, and this is her secret recipe. They are perfect as a main course, served with a nice salad on the side. For a super-sexy alternative, add some tuna to the ricotta stuffing and thank me later … *mamma mia!*

6 medium courgettes (zucchini)
drizzle of extra virgin olive oil
1 garlic clove, chopped
200 g (7 oz) ricotta
1 egg
80 g (3 oz/ 1 cup) breadcrumbs
small bunch of parsley
100 g (3½ oz) Parmesan cheese, grated (shredded)
50 g (2 oz) grated (shredded) mozzarella
salt and freshly ground black pepper

Preheat the oven to 180°C fan (400°F) and line a baking tray with baking parchment.

Halve the courgettes lengthways and scoop out the flesh using a spoon. Place your courgette 'shells' in the prepared tray and season generously with salt. Set aside.

Finely chop the scooped-out courgette flesh. Heat the oil in a frying pan (skillet) over a low–medium heat, then add the courgette flesh and garlic. Season with salt and pepper and cook for 15 minutes, stirring occasionally.

Tip the cooked courgette flesh into a food processor. Add the ricotta, egg, breadcrumbs and parsley, along with 80 g (3 oz) of the Parmesan, and whizz everything together for 30 seconds, or until creamy.

In the meantime, your courgette 'shells' should have released some moisture, so pat them dry with paper towels.

Scoop spoonfuls of your ricotta stuffing into the courgette 'shells', then sprinkle over the remaining Parmesan and bake for 35–40 minutes. Now sprinkle the grated mozzarella over the top and bake for a further 10 minutes, or until the cheese has fully melted. *Buon appetito!*

EASY ARANCINI

- SERVES -	- PREP TIME -	- COOK TIME -
6	30 minutes	25 minutes

Arancini (or *arancine* – there is a huge debate about the correct spelling in Italy) are Sicilian stuffed rice balls, traditionally filled with meat ragù, peas and cheese. Here, I want to show you a super-easy filling that is typical of the city of Palermo: béchamel sauce, ham and cheese! For a vegetarian alternative, simply replace the ham with some cooked spinach or mushrooms.

600 ml (20 fl oz/ 2½ cups) water
6 g (¼ oz/ 1 teaspoon) salt
250 g (9 oz/ scant 1¼ cups) risotto rice
1 teaspoon saffron
15 g (½ oz) unsalted butter
50 g (2 oz) Parmesan cheese, grated (shredded)
2 litres (70 fl oz/ 8 cups) sunflower oil, for deep-frying

- FOR THE FILLING -

250 ml (8½ fl oz/ 1 cup) Béchamel Sauce (see page 52; halve ingredients)
80 g (3 oz) cooked ham, finely chopped

Pour the water into a saucepan. Add the salt, and bring to the boil over a medium heat. Add the rice, then cover with a lid and cook for about 15 minutes or until al dente.

Meanwhile, soak the saffron in a couple of tablespoons of hot water and set aside.

Once the rice has cooked, it should have absorbed all the water. If not, drain any excess water. With the pan off the heat, add the saffron infusion to the rice, along with the butter and Parmesan. Mix all the ingredients together, then transfer the rice to a tray and spread it out evenly. Cover with cling film (plastic wrap) and leave to cool completely.

In a bowl, mix the béchamel sauce with the ham and mozzarella, then set aside.

Slightly wet your hands with some room-temperature water (this will prevent the rice from sticking to your hands as you work), then scoop up 2 tablespoons of the rice (about 80–100 g/ 3–3½ oz) and flatten it in one of your palms.

50 g (2 oz) grated (shredded) mozzarella or Provolone cheese, finely chopped

- FOR THE COATING -

50 g (2 oz/ scant ½ cup) plain (all-purpose) flour
100 ml (3½ fl oz/ scant ½ cup) water
pinch of salt
100 g (3½ oz/ 1¼ cups) breadcrumbs

Place ½ tablespoon of the cheese and ham mixture in the centre, then wrap the rice around it and form a ball, approximately 8 cm (3 in) in diameter. Set aside and repeat with the remaining rice and filling to make six rice balls.

To make the batter for the coating, mix together the flour, water and salt, and whisk until smooth. Scatter the breadcrumbs on a small plate. Dip each rice ball into the batter, letting any excess drip away, then roll in the breadcrumbs to coat. Set aside.

Pour the oil into a large, deep frying pan (skillet) over a high heat. Heat until the oil reaches 170°C (340°F). To check the oil is hot enough, simply dip the back of a wooden spoon in the oil and, if bubbles appear around it, you are ready to fry. Fry your arancini for about 7–8 minutes, or until golden brown. Serve while still warm. *Buon appetito!*

FRICO

- SERVES -	- PREP TIME -	- COOK TIME -
4	20 minutes	50 minutes

Frico is a typical dish of my region, Friuli-Venezia Giulia, where it is usually served during city festivals with roasted polenta or chips. It is the best comfort food ever; I like to describe it as a cheese and potato pancake. Traditionally, *frico* is made with Montasio cheese, but if you can't get hold of it, you can use a good-quality Cheddar instead.

drizzle of olive oil
1 large white onion, finely sliced
500 g (1 lb 2 oz) potatoes,
peeled and coarsely
grated (shredded)
250 g (9 oz) mild Montasio
cheese (or mild Cheddar), diced
250 g (9 oz) aged Montasio
cheese (or mature
Cheddar), diced
salt and freshly ground
black pepper

Heat the olive oil in a non-stick frying pan (skillet) over a low–medium heat. Add the onion and season with salt and pepper. Stir to combine, then cover with a lid and leave to cook for 10 minutes or until the onion has softened.

Stir in the grated potatoes, then cover with the lid once more and cook for another 15–20 minutes, stirring occasionally until you have a sticky and uniform paste.

Add the mild and aged cheeses, stir and leave to cook for 8–10 minutes, or until they are melted and well incorporated.

Make sure the mixture is covering the bottom of the pan in an even layer. Check the bottom crust is cooked by lifting it up slightly with your spoon – it should be a light brown colour.

Now it's time to cook the other side of the *frico*. Use a large round plate with a larger circumference than that of the pan. Set it on top of the pan, then, with a quick but careful movement, flip the plate and the pan together so the *frico* ends up on the plate. Slide the frico back into the pan to cook on the other side for 6–8 minutes, or until it has a light brown crust on the bottom. *Buon appetito!*

MY MUM'S MEATBALLS

- SERVES -	- PREP TIME -	- COOK TIME -
4–6	15 minutes	50 minutes

My mum makes the best meatballs ever, and I am so pleased to be sharing her secret recipe with you all. If you can find it, use minced (ground) rose veal instead of beef for a more delicate, lighter meatball. You can also add some sausage meat to the mixture for extra flavour. Serve these meatballs as a main course with some mashed potatoes on the side, or make them super small to garnish some pasta. *Buon appetito!*

80 g (3 oz) white bread, no crusts
milk, to cover
800 g (1 lb 12 oz) minced
(ground) beef
1 egg
small bunch of basil, chopped
30 g (1 oz) grated (shredded)
Parmesan cheese
salt and freshly ground
black pepper

- FOR THE TOMATO SAUCE -

generous drizzle of extra virgin
olive oil
1 small onion, finely chopped
1 garlic clove, finely chopped
400 g (14 oz) tin
peeled tomatoes

Place the bread in a bowl, then pour over enough milk to cover. Leave it to soak for 30 minutes.

Meanwhile, prepare your tomato sauce. Heat the olive oil in a saucepan over a low–medium heat. Add the onion and garlic and sizzle for a couple of minutes, then stir in the tomatoes. Season with salt and pepper to taste, then cook for 20 minutes, stirring occasionally.

Return to the bread. Remove it from the bowl and squeeze to remove excess milk, then add it to a large mixing bowl, along with the beef, egg, basil and cheese. Season with salt and pepper, then work the mixture together with your hands until amalgamated. Use your hands to roll it into small balls about the size of a table-tennis ball (this recipe should make approximately 40 balls).

Drop your meatballs into the tomato sauce and cook over a low–medium heat for 15–20 minutes, turning them halfway through. Serve warm with some mashed potatoes. *Buon appetito!*

VITELLO TONNATO

- SERVES -
4–6

- PREP TIME -
30 minutes, plus resting

- COOK TIME -
1 hour

Vitello tonnato is a classic dish of the Piedmont region: cold veal served with a tuna sauce. It might sound like a weird combination, but trust me, it's ... *mamma mia!* This is perfect for a summer dinner, a picnic or a delicious lunch at the beach.

1 kg (2 lb 4 oz) rose veal (silverside/ eye of round)
1 carrot, peeled and roughly chopped
1 celery stalk, roughly chopped
1 onion, peeled and halved
4 garlic cloves, peeled
5 cloves, lightly crushed
small bunch of rosemary
5 bay leaves
300 ml (10 fl oz/ 1¼ cups) white wine
room–temperature water, to cover
salt
handful of caper berries, to serve

Place the meat in a large pot. Add the carrot, celery, onion and garlic, along with the cloves, rosemary and bay leaves. Pour in the white wine, then add enough water to fully cover the meat. Season with salt, then place over a medium heat and bring to the boil.

Once the water starts to boil, reduce the heat to low, cover with a lid and cook for 1 hour (the rule is that every 500 g/1 lb 2 oz of meat needs 30 minutes of cooking).

After an hour, turn off the heat and leave the meat to rest in its broth for another hour (if you don't have time, you can skip this step). Do not discard the broth. You can use it for a lighter version of the tuna sauce (see *Sexy Tip*) or in risottos or soups.

- FOR THE TUNA SAUCE -

2 hard-boiled eggs, peeled
100 g (3½ oz) tinned tuna in
oil, drained
5 anchovy fillets
2 teaspoons salted capers
100 ml (3½ fl oz/ scant ½ cup)
extra virgin olive oil

- Sexy Tip -

For a lighter tuna sauce, replace
the extra virgin olive oil with the
same quantity of broth from
cooking the veal.

Remove the meat from the pan and wrap it in foil. Leave it to rest in the refrigerator for a couple of hours or overnight.

When you're almost ready to serve, it's time to make your tuna sauce. In a blender, combine the eggs, tuna, anchovies, capers and extra virgin olive oil, and blend for a minute or until smooth.

Remove the cold meat from the refrigerator and slice it thinly (approximately 2–3 mm thick) with a smooth-bladed knife. Arrange the slices on a plate, cover with the tuna sauce and top with the caper berries to serve. *Buon appetito!*

BOLOGNESE COTOLETTE

- SERVES -	- PREP TIME -	- COOK TIME -
4	10 minutes	20 minutes

Have you ever had Milanese *cotolette*? These are their sexier cousins – delicious fried veal escalopes, covered with Parma ham and cheese. Try replacing the Parma ham with mortadella for a delicious variation.

4 rose veal escalopes (scallops/cutlets), about 150–200 g (5–7 oz) each
2 medium eggs
pinch of ground nutmeg (or to taste)
100 g (3½ oz/ ¾ cup) plain (all-purpose) flour, plus 20 g (¾ oz/ scant ¼ cup) for the sauce
200 g (7 oz/ 2½ cups) breadcrumbs
150 g (5 oz) unsalted butter
4 large slices of Parma ham
150 g (5 oz) Parmesan cheese, grated (shredded)
200 ml (7 fl oz/ scant 1 cup) hot beef stock
salt and freshly ground black pepper

Beat the escalopes with a meat mallet to make them thin – approximately 3 mm.

Prepare three shallow bowls. In one, beat the eggs and season with the nutmeg and some salt and pepper. Add the flour to the second bowl, and the breadcrumbs to the third. One at a time, dip the escalopes first into the flour, then into the eggs and finally into the breadcrumbs to coat. Set aside.

Melt the butter in a large frying pan (skillet) over a low-medium heat. Add the coated escalopes and fry for 4–5 minutes on each side or until nice and golden. Lay a slice of Parma ham on top of each one, then sprinkle the grated Parmesan cheese on top. Add the hot beef stock to the pan, then cover with a lid and cook for a further 5 minutes, or until the cheese melts. Now transfer the meat to a serving plate.

Use a sieve to strain the cooking juices from the frying pan into a small saucepan. Place this over a high heat, add the 20 g (¾ oz/ scant ¼ cup) flour and whisk vigorously for about 3–4 minutes, or until it thickens into a sauce. Cover the escalopes with the sauce and serve. *Buon appetito!*

RICE-STUFFED TOMATOES

- SERVES -	- PREP TIME -	- COOK TIME -
4–6	15 minutes	1 hour 10 minutes

My nonna's stuffed tomatoes are the perfect idea for a summer dinner, and they are ready in just a few steps! You can add your favourite ingredients to the stuffing – try some basil pesto, tinned tuna or salami. For best results, I suggest using risotto rice for this recipe, as it contains more starches.

8 large tomatoes
drizzle of extra virgin olive oil
2 garlic cloves, finely chopped
1 teaspoon dried oregano
small bunch of parsley,
finely chopped
200 g (7 oz/ scant 1 cup) risotto
rice (arborio or carnaroli)
60 g (2 oz) Parmesan cheese,
grated (shredded)
100 g (3½ oz) Provolone
cheese, diced
small bunch of basil,
leaves picked
salt and freshly ground
black pepper

First, remove the tops from the tomatoes and set the tops aside. Using a teaspoon, carefully scoop out the pulp from inside the tomatoes. Add this to a blender and whizz for 30 seconds.

Place the 'empty' tomatoes on a wire rack over a plate. Salt generously, then turn them upside down so that excess liquid can drain out.

Heat the olive oil in a saucepan over a low–medium heat. Add the garlic and sizzle for a couple of minutes, then add the tomato pulp and oregano. Season with salt and pepper, and cook for 20 minutes.

Stir in the parsley, then turn off the heat and let the sauce cool slightly.

Preheat the oven to 180°C fan (400°F) and line a baking dish with baking parchment.

Bring a saucepan of salted water to the boil over a medium heat. Add the rice and cook until al dente (about 2–3 minutes less than the time indicated on the packaging). Drain, then tip the rice into a bowl. Add the tomato sauce, along with the Parmesan and half of the Provolone cheese. Stir to combine.

Spoon 2–3 tablespoons of the rice mixture into each 'empty' tomato, then add 4 cubes of Provolone cheese and cover with more rice until full. Place the stuffed tomatoes and the tomato tops alongside each other on the prepared dish and bake for 40–45 minutes, or until nice and golden.

Serve with some basil leaves scattered over the top. *Buon appetito!*

MY MUM'S CRISPY BEER CHICKEN

- SERVES -	- PREP TIME -	- COOK TIME -
4	5 minutes	1 hour

My mum always makes this dish at the weekend, serving it with roast potatoes. It's cosy, juicy and absolutely delicious! I love to make it on weeknights, when I don't have a lot of time to cook. You just add all the ingredients to a baking dish, chuck everything in the oven, and an hour later, your chicken is ready.

drizzle of extra virgin olive oil
8 chicken thighs, boneless, skin on
330 ml (11¼ fl oz/ 1⅓ cups) lager
2 garlic cloves, finely chopped
small bunch of rosemary, finely chopped
5 sage leaves, finely chopped
salt and freshly ground black pepper

Preheat the oven to 180°C fan (400°F).

Drizzle the olive oil into a large baking dish, then add your chicken thighs, skin-side down. Pour over the beer and season with salt and pepper, then scatter over your chopped garlic and herbs. Cover with foil and bake for 30 minutes.

Remove the foil, turn over the chicken so it's skin-side up, and bake uncovered for a further 30 minutes until golden and crispy. Spoon some of the beery sauce on top to serve. *Buon appetito!*

- Sexy Tip -

Try this recipe with white wine instead of beer: same measurements, different flavour, same super-sexy result!

CRISPY BAKED CALAMARI

- SERVES -	- PREP TIME -	- COOK TIME -
4	10 minutes	30 minutes

If you have no time to make dinner and you want to eat something delicious, you have to try these super-easy calamari. All you have to do is to mix all the ingredients in a bowl and bake. Easy, quick and, *mamma mia*, so good!

800 g (1 lb 12 oz) squid, skins removed
1 red onion, sliced
150 g (5 oz) cherry tomatoes, halved
100 g (3½ oz/ generous ¾ cup) pitted black olives
2 garlic cloves, chopped
50 g (2 oz) Parmesan cheese, grated (shredded)
zest and juice of 1 lemon
120 g (4 oz/ 1½ cups) breadcrumbs
drizzle of olive oil
small bunch of parsley, chopped
salt

Preheat the oven to 180°C fan (400°F) and line a baking tray with baking parchment.

Wash and dry your squid. Remove the central 'bone', then cut the squid tube into 1 cm (½ in) rings and chop the tentacles into pieces. Add to a bowl.

Add the onion, cherry tomatoes, olives, garlic, Parmesan cheese, lemon zest and breadcrumbs. Drizzle with olive oil, season with salt and mix with your hands until well combined.

Tip this mixture on to the prepared baking tray and spread it out evenly. Drizzle over some more oil, then bake for 25–30 minutes, or until your calamari are nice and crispy.

To serve, squeeze over some lemon juice and top with some parsley. *Buon appetito!*

- Sexy Tip -

Serve your calamari with truffle mayonnaise for extra sexiness!

PANZEROTTI

- MAKES -	- PREP TIME -	- COOK TIME -
10–12	30 minutes, plus resting	15 minutes

Panzerotti are delicious pizza pockets typical of the Puglia region. They are super easy to make, and you can stuff them with your favourite filling. Try ricotta and salami, pesto and mozzarella, or mushrooms and smoked cheese ... *mamma mia!*

500 g (1 lb 2 oz/ 4 cups) plain (all-purpose) flour, plus extra for dusting

3 g (⅛ teaspoon) fast-action dried yeast

5 g (1 teaspoon) caster (superfine) sugar

290 ml (9¾ fl oz/scant 1¼ cups) lukewarm water

10 g (½ oz/ 2 teaspoons) salt

15 ml (1 tablespoon) extra virgin olive oil

2 litres (70 fl oz/ 8 cups) sunflower oil, for deep-frying

- FOR THE FILLING -

250 g (9 oz) tomato passata (sieved tomatoes)

In a large bowl, mix together the flour, yeast and sugar. Add half of the lukewarm water and mix with a wooden spoon. Once incorporated, add the salt and remaining water, and continue working the dough for another minute or until all the ingredients come together. Add the olive oil and start kneading the dough with your hands for a couple of minutes, then transfer it to a clean surface and knead it for 2–3 minutes more, or until you have a smooth dough.

Roll out your dough into a sausage shape and cut it into 10–12 pieces of about 70–80 g (2¼–3 oz) each. Shape each piece into a ball, then place these dough balls on a tray. Cover with cling film (plastic wrap) and leave to rest for a couple of hours.

Meanwhile, let's prepare the filling. In a bowl, combine the tomato passata with the oregano and olive oil. Season with salt and pepper, then stir in the mozzarella cubes. Set aside.

After 2 hours, transfer your dough balls to a lightly floured surface and roll out each one with a rolling pin to create discs about 2–3 mm thick.

1 teaspoon dried oregano
drizzle of extra virgin olive oil
300 g (10½ oz) grated
(shredded) mozzarella
salt and freshly ground
black pepper

- Sexy Tip -

Instead of frying, you can bake
your *panzerotti* in the oven at
200°C fan (425°F) for about 20
minutes, or until nice and golden.

Place 1 tablespoon of your tomato and mozzarella filling in the centre of each disc, then fold the discs in half to create a half-moon shape. Press down the edges with your fingers or the tines of a fork so the filling does not come out while your panzerotti are frying.

Pour the sunflower oil into a large, deep frying pan (skillet) over a high heat. Heat until the oil reaches 170°C (340°F). To check the oil is hot enough, simply dip the back of a wooden spoon in the oil and, if bubbles appear around it, you are ready to fry. Fry your *panzerotti* 2–3 at a time for a couple of minutes on each side, or until nice and golden. Drain on a plate lined with paper towels, and serve hot. *Buon appetito!*

SICILIAN COD

I learned this dish from Carlo, a Sicilian fishmonger whom I met while on holiday in Palermo a few years ago. I was looking for a quick recipe for dinner, and he immediately suggested this recipe, which he always makes for his own family. It is super easy and quick to make. You can flour the fish before adding it to the pan for extra sexiness.

drizzle of extra virgin olive oil
1 garlic clove, chopped
250 g (9 oz) cherry tomatoes, halved
2 medium potatoes, peeled and finely diced
250 g (9 oz) tomato passata (sieved tomatoes)
100 ml (3½ fl oz/ scant ½ cup) water
4 skinless cod fillets (about 125–150 g/4–5 oz each)
20 g (¾ oz/ scant ¼ cup) green or black olives, pitted
small bunch of parsley, chopped
salt and freshly ground black pepper

Heat the olive oil in large frying pan (skillet) over a low–medium heat. Add the garlic and cherry tomatoes and cook for a couple of minutes, then add the potatoes, tomato passata and water. Season with salt and pepper, then cover with a lid and cook for about 20–25 minutes, stirring occasionally, until the potatoes are nice and soft.

Add your cod fillets to the pan, scatter the olives on top, then cover once more and cook for a further 10 minutes, or until the fish is fully cooked (the cooking time may vary depending on the size of the fish).

Serve topped with parsley. *Buon appetito!*

POTATO GATEAU

Potato gateau was created in Naples towards the end of the 18th century. After a brief holiday in France, the Queen of Naples asked her chefs to prepare a potato dish using local ingredients she had tasted during her visit. Potato gateau was born. Think of it as a cheesy mashed potato lasagne – it's *mamma mia!*

40 g (1½ oz) unsalted butter
40 g (1½ oz/ ½ cup) breadcrumbs
1 kg (2 lb 4 oz) potatoes, peeled and chopped
2 eggs
90 g (3¼ oz) Parmesan cheese, grated (shredded)
pinch of ground nutmeg
60 ml (2 fl oz/ ¼ cup) milk
180 g (6½ oz) Provolone cheese, diced
160 g (5¾ oz) Italian salami, diced
salt and freshly ground black pepper

Preheat the oven to 180°C fan (400°F). Grease the bottom of a baking dish with 20 g (¾ oz) of the butter, then scatter over 20 g (¾ oz/¼ cup) of your breadcrumbs. Set aside.

Bring a large saucepan of salted water to the boil. Add the potatoes and boil for about 20 minutes or until tender. Drain, then tip into a bowl and mash them with a potato ricer.

Add the eggs to the bowl, along with 60 g (2 oz) of the Parmesan. Season with the nutmeg and salt and pepper to taste, then start stirring in the milk, adding it a little at a time. Once it's all incorporated, stir in the Provolone cheese and salami. The texture of the mixture should be quite solid.

Pour the potato mixture into the prepared baking dish and level it. Sprinkle over the remaining breadcrumbs, along with the rest of the Parmesan. Cube the remaining butter and scatter that over the top.

Cover the whole thing with foil and bake for 40 minutes.

Towards the end of the cooking time, remove the foil. Then, for the last 5 minutes or so, transfer the dish to under a hot grill (broiler) to finish it off and form a crust.

Let your potato gateau rest on the side for 10 minutes before serving. *Buon appetito!*

DOLCI

DOLCI

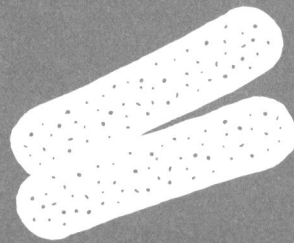

D

DOLCI

DOLCI

OLCI

DOLCI

The perfect meal always ends with a delicious dessert, and in this chapter, you will learn how to make the best Italian desserts! From cakes to gelato to homemade chocolate hazelnut spread, get ready to eat like there is no tomorrow. And it's not just about dessert – did you know that in Italy, we actually have cake for breakfast? Make yourself a nice cup of coffee and start your day in a super-sexy way!

I often get asked what's my favourite dessert ever, and although I adore every single recipe in this chapter, I must admit that nothing can beat a good tiramisù. The one in this cookbook is my aunt's Mara recipe, so it has a special place in my heart.

MAMMA
Mia!

CREAMY CLASSIC TIRAMISÙ

- SERVES -	- PREP TIME -	- CHILL TIME -
6	30 minutes	2+ hours

OK, I have to admit it: this is not the original recipe for tiramisù (it is my Aunt Mara's and it is one that I cherish dearly) – but it is definitely the sexiest one! The original recipe does not contain cream, but this one does – and it is the version that most Italians use nowadays. Tiramisù literally means 'pick me up' in Italian, and the legend goes that it was invented in the 1800s by a mistress of a 'house of pleasures' in Treviso in the north-east of Italy, as a gift to her customers after a strenuous session.

3 eggs, separated
250 ml (8½ fl oz/ 1 cup) double (heavy) cream, cold
3 tablespoons caster (superfine) sugar
500 g (1 lb 2 oz) mascarpone
250 ml (8½ fl oz/ 1 cup) coffee, cooled
200 g (7 oz) ladyfingers or Savoiardi biscuits
30g (1 oz/ ¼ cup) unsweetened cocoa, plus extra to decorate

In a small bowl, whisk your egg whites with an electric mixer for a couple of minutes, or until firm. Set aside.

In another bowl, whip the double cream for a couple of minutes, or until firm. Set aside.

In a third bowl, whisk the egg yolks with the sugar for 90 seconds, then add the mascarpone and mix until creamy. Add your whipped cream and whisked egg whites, little by little, and mix everything for a couple of minutes.

Pour your cooled coffee into a shallow dish. Dip the ladyfinger biscuits into the coffee for a couple of seconds on each side. Arrange half of these soaked biscuits in the base of a shallow 20 × 30 cm (8 × 12 in) dish. Spread half of your tiramisù cream on top, then sprinkle over half of the cocoa powder. Repeat this layering process with the remaining ingredients.

Let your tiramisù rest in the refrigerator for at least a couple of hours (even better overnight), and decorate with some more cocoa powder on top before serving. *Buon appetito!*

TORTA PARADISO

- SERVES -	- PREP TIME -	- COOK TIME -
6	15 minutes	40 minutes

This 'paradise cake' is the softest, most beautifully light cake you will ever taste in your life, and it is made with just a few simple ingredients that you probably already have at home! Legend has it that this cake was invented by a pastry chef in the Lombardy region, and that it was given its iconic name after a customer tasted it and exclaimed, 'This cake is paradise!'

120 g (4 oz) unsalted butter, at room temperature
190 g (6½ oz/ generous ¾ cup) caster (superfine) sugar
4 eggs
zest of 1 lemon
180 g (6½ oz/ 1½ cups) plain (all-purpose) flour
100 g (3½ oz/generous ¾ cup) potato starch
15 g (1 tablespoon) baking powder
1 tablespoon icing (confectioners') sugar, to finish

Preheat the oven to 180°C fan (400°F) and line a 22 cm (8½ in) round cake tin (pan) with baking parchment.

In a mixing bowl, combine the butter with the caster sugar and whisk together with a hand mixer for about 5 minutes, or until you have a super-soft paste.

Incorporate the eggs one by one, mixing between each addition, then add the lemon zest and keep whisking for a couple more minutes.

Now sift in the flour, potato starch and baking powder, then mix everything together for another minute or until smooth.

Pour the batter into the prepared tin and bake in the oven for about 40 minutes, or until a skewer inserted into the middle comes out clean.

Leave to cool in the tin, then serve with icing sugar sprinkled on top. *Buon appetito!*

THREE-INGREDIENT GELATO

- SERVES -	- PREP TIME -	- FREEZING TIME -
6–8	5 minutes	2+ hours

Have you ever wanted to make your own gelato at home, but you don't own one of those super-fancy and expensive gelato machines? Don't worry – I've got you covered! My super-easy gelato recipe only requires three ingredients, and it will take you less than five minutes to prepare it. Then just freeze it for two hours and you will have your own homemade gelato that will make you whisper ... *mamma mia!*

250 g (9 oz) dark chocolate, finely chopped
500 ml (17 fl oz/ 2 cups) double (heavy) cream, very cold from the refrigerator
350 g (12 oz/ generous 1 cup) condensed milk

Place the dark chocolate in a heatproof bowl and melt in the microwave for three bursts of 30 seconds each, giving it a stir each time to prevent the chocolate from burning. Set aside to cool.

Meanwhile, take your double cream out of the refrigerator and pour it into a mixing bowl. Whip with a hand mixer until soft peaks form and it becomes nice and fluffy.

Fold the condensed milk and cooled melted chocolate into the cream, and gently mix everything together until smooth. Transfer the chocolate cream to a freezer-proof container and freeze for 2 hours. Then it's ready for you to enjoy. *Buon appetito!*

- *Sexy Tip* -

Make your own gelato flavour by replacing the dark chocolate with some strawberry purée, pistachio cream or lemon juice.

MASCARPONE APPLE CAKE

- SERVES -	- PREP TIME -	- COOK TIME -
6	15 minutes	45 minutes

Did you know that in Italy, we eat cake for breakfast? I don't know why, but this surprises a lot of my friends every time I say it. If you'd like to try an Italian breakfast, start with this delicious apple cake. It is super soft, light and moist, and is perfect dipped in some hot tea!

6 apples, cored
juice of 2 lemons
4 medium eggs
180 g (6½ oz/ generous ¾ cup) caster (superfine) sugar, plus 1 tablespoon to sprinkle on top
250 g (9 oz) mascarpone cheese
pinch of salt
200 g (7 oz/ generous 1½ cups) plain (all-purpose) flour
12 g (½ oz) baking powder
1 teaspoon ground cinnamon
2 tablespoons icing (confectioners') sugar, to finish

Preheat the oven to 180°C fan (400°F) and line a 22 cm (8½ in) round cake tin (pan) with baking parchment.

Dice three of your apples into small cubes, and slice the remaining three into thin slices about 2 mm thick. Put the apple cubes into one shallow bowl and the slices into another, then pour over the lemon juice and give them each a nice mix (this will prevent the apples from turning brown).

Break the eggs into a mixing bowl. Add the 180 g (6½ oz/ generous ¾ cup) caster sugar and mix with a hand mixer for 1 minute. Add the mascarpone and salt, and mix for a further 20 seconds. Sift in the flour, baking powder and cinnamon, and mix everything for another minute or until smooth.

Drain your apple cubes in a colander to remove any excess lemon juice, then add them to the cake mixture. Stir with a spoon until the apples are well incorporated, then pour the cake batter into the prepared tin.

Drain your apple slices in the colander to remove any excess lemon juice, then arrange them on top of your cake. Sprinkle the 1 tablespoon of caster sugar on top, then bake for 40–45 minutes until golden brown and a skewer inserted into the cake comes out clean.

Let your cake cool completely in the tin, then serve with icing sugar sprinkled on top. *Buon appetito!*

BLUEBERRY RICOTTA CAKE

- SERVES -	- PREP TIME -	- COOK TIME -
6	15 minutes	1 hour

This is probably my favourite cake ever. It's perfect for any occasion, it's extremely soft and moist, and it's super easy to make!

3 eggs
250 g (9 oz) ricotta
1 teaspoon vanilla extract
zest of 1 lemon and juice of ½
200 g (7 oz/ scant 1 cup) caster (superfine) sugar
pinch of salt
200 g (7 oz/ generous 1½ cups) plain (all-purpose) flour, plus 1 tablespoon for the blueberries
2 teaspoons baking powder
100 g (3½ oz) unsalted butter, melted
250 g (9 oz) fresh blueberries
2 tablespoons icing (confectioners') sugar, to finish

- Sexy Tip -

Try this cake with strawberries, raspberries and blackberries. You could even try mixing all your favourite berries together!

Preheat the oven to 180°C fan (400°F) and line a 22 cm (8½ in) round cake tin (pan) with baking parchment.

Break the eggs into a mixing bowl, then add the ricotta, vanilla and lemon zest and juice. Whisk together with a hand mixer for a minute or until smooth. Add the caster sugar and salt and whisk for a couple of minutes more, then sift in the flour and baking powder, and whisk for another minute. Finally, add the melted butter and whisk once more until you have a nice, silky batter.

Tip 200 g (7 oz) of your blueberries into a small bowl and scatter over the 1 tablespoon of flour. Mix with a spoon to coat your blueberries evenly. This will prevent them from sinking when baking.

Mix the floured blueberries into the cake batter, then pour it into the prepared cake tin. Top with the remaining blueberries (not coated with flour) and bake for 50–60 minutes until golden brown and a skewer inserted in the centre comes out clean.

Let your cake cool completely in the tin, then serve with icing sugar sprinkled on top.

CAMILLE

- SERVES -	- PREP TIME -	- COOK TIME -
10–12	15 minutes	20 minutes

Camille are mini carrot cakes, and they are the typical dessert that Italian parents make for their kids to take to school. This recipe makes 10–12 *camille*, depending on the size of your muffin moulds. You can add some chopped nuts to the carrot mixture for some extra crunchiness!

2 medium eggs
220 g (7¾ oz/ scant 1 cup) caster (superfine) sugar
350 g (12 oz) carrots, peeled and finely grated (shredded)
100 ml (3½ fl oz/ scant ½ cup) olive oil
100 ml (3½ fl oz/ scant ½ cup) freshly squeezed orange juice
zest of 2 oranges
1 teaspoon vanilla extract
100 g (3½ oz/ 1 cup) almond flour
280 g (10 oz/ 2¼ cups) plain (all-purpose) flour
2 teaspoons baking powder

Preheat the oven to 180°C fan (400°F) and line a muffin tray with paper cases.

In a mixing bowl, whisk the eggs and caster sugar with a hand mixer for a couple of minutes until you have a fluffy mixture. Add the grated carrots, olive oil, orange juice, orange zest, vanilla and almond flour and stir, then sift in the plain flour and baking powder. Mix all the ingredients together until smooth.

Divide the batter between the muffin cases, making sure you don't overfill them – the mixture needs to stay 1.5 cm (⅝ in) below the edge of the cases. Bake for 20 minutes until nice and golden.

Let your *camille* cool in the tray, then serve. *Buon appetito!*

HOMEMADE CHOCOLATE HAZELNUT CREAM

- SERVES -	- PREP TIME -	- COOK TIME -
6–8	15 minutes	10 minutes

Did you know that you can make a delicious hazelnut cream at home in just a few steps? Spread it on top of some bread, drizzle it on some gelato or use it to decorate your cakes to make them ... *mamma mia!*

100 g (3½ oz/ scant ¾ cup) hazelnuts
100 g (3½ oz/ scant ½ cup) caster (superfine) sugar
150 g (5 oz) milk chocolate, chopped into small pieces
150 g (5 oz) dark chocolate, chopped into small pieces
180 ml (6 fl oz/ ¾ cup) milk, warm
3 tablespoons sunflower oil

- *Sexy Tip* -

To sterilise your jars, wash them and the lids in hot soapy water. Leave them to stand upside down on a roasting tray, then pop the tray in a preheated oven at 160–180°C fan (350– 400°F) for 15 minutes.

Toast the hazelnuts in a non-stick frying pan (skillet) over a medium heat for about 5 minutes, then let them cool.

Add the toasted hazelnuts to a food processor, along with the sugar, milk chocolate and dark chocolate. Whizz everything together for 2–3 minutes or until floury in consistency.

Add the warm milk a little at a time, mixing between each addition, then add the oil. Keep blitzing for a couple of minutes, or until you have a smooth cream.

Bring a saucepan of water to the boil and set a heatproof bowl on top, ensuring that the bottom of the bowl does not touch the boiling water. Pour your homemade hazelnut cream into the heatproof bowl, then stir continuously for 5 minutes without allowing it to boil.

Transfer the hazelnut cream to a sterilised glass jar and allow it to cool completely before sealing with a lid. *Buon appetito!*

MY DAD'S BUTTERNUT SQUASH CAKE

This butternut squash cake recipe is my dad's pride and joy. He makes it all the time, and he believes that he is the only one in the family who can make it perfectly. I hope I can do him justice here!

75 ml (2½ fl oz/ 5 tablespoons) milk
170 g (6 oz/ ¾ cup) caster (superfine) sugar
100 ml (3½ fl oz/ scant ½ cup) olive oil
2 teaspoons vanilla extract
2 teaspoons ground cinnamon
300 g (10½ oz) butternut squash flesh, grated (shredded)
250 g (9 oz/ 2 cups) plain (all-purpose) flour
8 g (¼ oz) baking powder
40 g (1½ oz/ scant ¼ cup) chocolate chips
70 g (2¼ oz/ ¾ cup) walnuts, chopped
pinch of salt

Preheat the oven to 180°C fan (400°F) and line a 21 × 11 cm (8 × 4 in) loaf tin (pan) with baking parchment.

In a mixing bowl, combine the milk, caster sugar, oil, vanilla and cinnamon, and whisk by hand for a couple of minutes or until smooth. Stir in the grated squash, then sift in the flour and baking powder, and stir. Add the chocolate chips, walnuts and salt, and mix to combine. Transfer the cake mixture to the prepared tin.

Bake for 40–45 minutes, until a skewer inserted into the middle comes out clean.

Remove the cake from the oven and allow to cool in the tin. Serve with walnuts and a drizzle of icing on top if you like – *buon appetito!*

STRAWBERRY PANNA COTTA

- SERVES -	- PREP TIME -	- COOK TIME -
4	5 minutes	20 minutes, plus setting

Panna cotta literally means 'cooked cream' in Italian, and it is my go-to dessert when I have guests over for dinner. It can be prepared the night before, ready to serve to your guests the day after!

8 g (⅓ oz) gelatine sheets
500 ml (17 fl oz/ 2 cups) double (heavy) cream
90 g (3¼ oz/ generous ⅓ cup) caster (superfine) sugar
2 teaspoons vanilla extract

- FOR THE SAUCE -

150 g (5 oz) strawberries, chopped
20 g (¾ oz/ 1½ tablespoons) caster (superfine) sugar
10 ml (2 teaspoons) lemon juice
zest of ½ lemon

- Sexy Tip -

Try different toppings for your panna cotta. Chocolate, caramel or wild berries will all work wonderfully!

Place the gelatine sheets in a bowl and add enough room-temperature water to cover. Set aside.

In a saucepan over a low heat, combine the double cream, sugar and vanilla. Stir and bring to a simmer. When you see some little bubbles appearing, remove the saucepan from the heat. Drain your softened gelatine sheets and add to the pan, stirring until they completely dissolve.

Pour the panna cotta mixture into four glasses and leave to set in the refrigerator for a couple of hours.

In the meantime, prepare your strawberry sauce. In a small saucepan over a low–medium heat, combine the chopped strawberries, sugar, lemon juice and zest. Cook for 15 minutes, then allow to cool.

Serve your panna cotta topped with the strawberry sauce. *Buon appetito!*

CHOCOLATE AND VANILLA BUNDT CAKE

- SERVES -	- PREP TIME -	- COOK TIME -
6	20 minutes	45 minutes

My mum started making this cake when she was diagnosed as lactose intolerant, and it immediately became one of our family's favourite cakes. If you don't own a Bundt tin, you can absolutely make it in a normal cake tin or loaf tin.

120ml (4 fl oz/ ½ cup) sunflower oil, plus extra for greasing

350 g (12 oz/ 2¾ cups) plain (all-purpose) flour, plus extra for dusting

4 medium eggs

220 g (7¾ oz/ scant 1 cup) caster (superfine) sugar

3 teaspoons vanilla extract

120 ml (4 fl oz/ ½ cup) room temperature water

15 g (½ oz/ 1 tablespoon) baking powder

30 g (1 oz/ ¼ cup) unsweetened cocoa powder

2 tablespoons icing (confectioners') sugar, to finish

Preheat the oven to 180°C fan (400°F), and grease and flour a 24 cm (9½ in) Bundt tin (pan).

In a mixing bowl, whisk the eggs and sugar with a hand mixer for about 90 seconds, or until fluffy. Add the vanilla extract, room-temperature water and sunflower oil, and whisk for another minute. Sift in the flour and baking powder and mix one last time.

Pour half of the mixture into the prepared Bundt tin, then add the cocoa powder to the remaining mixture in the bowl. Mix well, then pour the chocolate mixture into the Bundt tin on top of the vanilla mixture.

Bake for 40–45 minutes, until a skewer inserted into the centre comes out clean.

Turn the cake out on to a wire rack and allow to cool before serving with a dusting of icing sugar.

LIMONCELLO TIRAMISÙ

- SERVES -	- PREP TIME -	- CHILL TIME -
6	30 minutes	2+ hours

I made this limoncello tiramisù for the first time a few years ago for my best friend Serxhio's birthday, and it was a huge success! It is so fresh and creamy: the perfect ending to a nice summer dinner. For best results, always let your tiramisù rest in the refrigerator overnight. For a variation, try replacing the lemons with oranges.

250 g (9 oz) ladyfingers or Savoiardi biscuits
lemon slices, to decorate

- FOR THE LIMONCELLO DIP -

70 g (2¼ oz/ scant ⅓ cup) caster (superfine) sugar
zest of 1 lemon
20 ml (1½ tablespoons) limoncello

- FOR THE TIRAMISU CREAM -

500 g (1 lb 2 oz) mascarpone
50 g (2 oz/ scant ½ cup) icing (confectioners') sugar
200 ml (7 fl oz/ scant 1 cup) double (heavy) cream, cold
zest and juice of 1 lemon
10 ml (2 teaspoons) limoncello

Begin by making the limoncello dip. In a small saucepan over a low–medium heat, combine the sugar, 400 ml (14 fl oz/ generous 1½ cups) water and lemon zest. Mix everything together and bring to the boil, then take off the heat and pour into a shallow bowl. Leave to cool completely, then pour in the limoncello. Set side.

To make the mascarpone cream, combine the mascarpone and icing sugar in a large bowl and mix with a hand mixer for 1 minute. Still mixing, pour in the double cream a little at a time, the lemon zest and juice and the limoncello. Keep mixing for another 90 seconds until a smooth cream forms. Set aside.

To assemble the tiramisù, dip the ladyfingers into the limoncello dip for a couple of seconds on each side, then arrange half of these soaked biscuits in the base of a shallow 20 × 30 cm (8 × 12 in) dish. Spread half of your tiramisù cream on top and repeat this layering until the ingredients are all used up.

Let your limoncello tiramisù rest in the refrigerator for a couple of hours – or, even better, overnight – and decorate with some lemon slices on top to serve. *Buon appetito!*

OLIVE OIL CAKE

- SERVES -	- PREP TIME -	- COOK TIME -
6	10 minutes	50 minutes

It's soft, it's moist and it smells like heaven – it must be my super-easy olive oil cake! For this recipe, I suggest using regular olive oil rather than extra virgin, as that would be too strong in flavour. You can make this cake just as it is, but sometimes I use it as the basis for other recipes: try adding some orange juice to the batter and covering it with orange slices for a quick orange cake, or adding some diced apples to make the softest apple cake of your life ... *mamma mia!*

150 g (5 oz/ scant ¾ cup) olive oil

170 g (6 oz/ ¾ cup) caster (superfine) sugar

3 medium eggs

150 ml (5 fl oz/ scant ⅔ cup) milk, at room temperature

zest of 1 lemon

300 g (10½ oz/ scant 2½ cups) plain (all-purpose) flour

15 g (1 tablespoon) baking powder

icing (confectioners') sugar, to finish

Preheat the oven to 180°C fan (400°F) and line a 20 × 15 cm (8 × 6 in) cake tin (pan) with baking parchment.

In a mixing bowl, combine the olive oil and caster sugar and whisk with a hand mixer for 90 seconds or until smooth. Incorporate the eggs one at a time, mixing between each addition, then add the milk and lemon zest and mix again. Sift in the flour and baking powder and mix once more to combine.

Transfer the mixture to the prepared tin, then bake for 45–50 minutes until a skewer inserted into the middle of the cake comes out clean.

Allow to cool in the tin, then serve your olive oil cake with some icing sugar sprinkled on top and enjoy. *Buon appetito!*

CHOCOLATE SALAMI

- SERVES -	- PREP TIME -	- CHILL TIME -
4	10 minutes	3+ hours

I still remember when I made chocolate salami for the very first time ... I was eight years old, and my Italian teacher Giuliana handed us a piece of paper at the end of class with her 'secret recipe for the easiest dessert ever'. That same day, I went home and made this mysterious dessert with my mum, and it was the best thing I had ever tasted in my life! Twenty years later, I still use my teacher's recipe; I have just added a bit of coffee to the original version to make it even sexier!

200 g (7 oz) dark chocolate, finely chopped
100 g (3½ oz) unsalted butter, at room temperature
150 g (5 oz/ generous ⅔ cup) caster (superfine) sugar
10 ml (2 teaspoons) coffee (or rum!)
20 g (¾ oz/ scant ¼ cup) unsweetened cocoa powder
120 g (4 oz) plain biscuits (cookies)
icing (confectioners') sugar, to finish

– Sexy Tip –

Why not add some chopped pistachios or hazelnuts to your chocolate mix for some added crunch?

Place the chocolate in a heatproof bowl and melt it in the microwave on high in three to four 20–second bursts, stirring between each one. Set aside to cool.

In a mixing bowl, mix the butter and caster sugar with a hand mixer for about 90 seconds, or until you have a creamy consistency. Add the cooled melted chocolate, along with the coffee and cocoa powder, and mix everything together for another 30 seconds, or until smooth.

Place your biscuits in a Ziplock bag and bash them with a rolling pin to roughly crush. Stir the crushed biscuits into the chocolate mixture.

Spread out a sheet of baking parchment or cling film (plastic wrap) on your work surface, then tip the chocolate mixture on to it. Use the parchment or cling film to roll it into a big sausage shape, and wrap this in the parchment or cling film.

Chill your chocolate salami in the refrigerator for at least 3 hours, before serving with a dusting of icing sugar on top.

MY NONNA'S LEMON TART

- SERVES -	- PREP TIME -	- COOK TIME -
6	30 minutes, plus resting	40 minutes

I grew up with my *nonna* making this tart every summer. Her friend Lucia used to come back from her regular holidays on the Amalfi Coast with a lot of lemons from Sorrento, which she always gifted to her friends. My *nonna* used most of them to make limoncello, but she always saved a few to make this lemon tart.

- FOR THE PASTRY -

200 g (7 oz/ generous 1½ cups)
plain (all-purpose) flour, plus
extra for dusting
100 g (3½ oz/ generous ¾ cup)
potato starch
5 g (¼ oz/ 1 teaspoon)
baking powder
180 g (6½ oz/ generous ¾ cup)
caster (superfine) sugar
150 g (5 oz) unsalted butter,
cubed, cold
1 medium egg
pinch of salt
zest of 2 lemons
15 ml (2½ teaspoons)
lemon juice

Begin by preparing the pastry. Sift the flour, potato starch and baking powder into a mixing bowl. Add the sugar, butter, egg and salt, along with the lemon zest and juice. Mix all the ingredients together with a spoon, then knead for a couple of minutes until a smooth dough forms. Wrap the dough in cling film (plastic wrap) and rest in the refrigerator for 30 minutes.

Meanwhile, preheat the oven to 180°C fan (400°F) and prepare the lemon cream. Break the eggs into a clean mixing bowl, then add the sugar, milk and cornflour, along with the lemon zest and juice. Whisk all the ingredients together to combine, then pour the mixture into a small saucepan over a low heat. Bring to a simmer, stirring, and cook for about 5–10 minutes, or until the sauce thickens. Turn off the heat and allow to cool.

Remove your pastry from the refrigerator and cut off two-thirds of it. Using a rolling pin, roll this out on a lightly floured surface to a round shape about 3 mm thick, then use it to line a 24 cm (9½ in)tart tin (pan), pressing down gently to fit it into the tin. Trim and remove any excess dough. Prick the bottom of the dough with a fork, then pour in the lemon cream.

- FOR THE LEMON CREAM -

2 medium eggs
160 g (5¼ oz/ scant ¾ cup)
caster (superfine) sugar
400 ml (14 fl oz/ generous
1½ cups) milk
50 g (2 oz/ scant ½ cup)
cornflour (cornstarch)
zest of 2 lemons
3 tablespoons lemon juice

- TO SERVE -

icing (confectioners') sugar,
for dusting

Roll out the remaining dough to about 3 mm thick, then cut into approximately 11 strips. Arrange these on top of the tart in a criss–cross pattern. Bake for about 40 minutes, or until the top is light brown in colour.

Serve dusted with icing sugar, and enjoy!

CAPRESE CAKE

- SERVES -
4–6

- PREP TIME -
15 minutes

- COOK TIME -
45 minutes

I like to define *caprese* cake as the Italian brownie. It was invented in 1920 by a pastry chef from the island of Capri. The story goes that he accidentally forgot to add the flour when he was mixing his cake mixture, but the resulting bake was so delicious that it became the signature dessert of the island!

300 g (10½ oz) dark chocolate, finely chopped
220 g (7¾ oz) unsalted butter
5 large eggs, separated
pinch of salt
220 g (7¾ oz/ scant 1 cup) caster (superfine) sugar
150 g (5 oz/ 1½ cups) almond flour
1 teaspoon vanilla extract
icing (confectioners') sugar, to finish

Preheat the oven to 170°C fan (375°F) and line a 22 cm (8½ in) baking tin with baking parchment.

Place the chocolate and butter in a heatproof bowl and melt in the microwave on high in three to four 20-second bursts, stirring between each one. Set aside to cool.

In a large bowl, whisk the egg whites with the salt for a couple of minutes or until firm.

In another bowl, combine the egg yolks and the caster sugar and whisk with a hand mixer for a couple of minutes until fluffy. Add the melted chocolate and butter mixture, along with the almond flour and vanilla, and mix everything until smooth.

Gently fold your whisked egg whites into this mixture, then transfer to the prepared tin. Bake for 45 minutes until the top of the cake starts to crack and a skewer inserted into the centre comes out pretty clean.

Allow to cool in the tin, then serve with some icing sugar dusted on top. *Buon appetito!*

THREE-INGREDIENT LEMON MOUSSE

- SERVES -
4

- PREP TIME -
5 minutes

If you're looking for the quickest dessert ever, you have to try this three-ingredient lemon mousse! Serve it alone in a glass, or use it to decorate cakes or cupcakes. You can replace the lemons with oranges for a super-sexy alternative!

80 g (3 oz/ scant ⅔ cup) icing (confectioners') sugar
zest and juice of 2 lemons
300 ml (10 fl oz/ 1¼ cups) double (heavy) cream, cold

In a mixing bowl, combine the icing sugar and lemon juice, and mix with a hand mixer for 1 minute. Add the double cream (make sure it's very cold) and whip everything together for about 90 seconds, or until you have a nice fluffy texture (make sure you don't overwhip it).

Divide your lemon mousse between four small glasses and top with some lemon zest to decorate. *Buon appetito!*

PISTACHIO LAVA CAKE

- SERVES -	- PREP TIME -	- COOK TIME -
4	15 minutes	17 minutes

If you like chocolate lava cake, you will love my super-easy pistachio version! This is another great dessert for when you have guests coming over for dinner, as you can prepare it the day before, store it in the refrigerator and simply bake it just before serving. If you like, you can replace the pistachio cream with some hazelnut cream (see page 135) for a version that will make you whisper ... *mamma mia!*

60 g (2 oz) unsalted butter, plus extra for greasing
50 g (2 oz/ scant ½ cup) plain (all-purpose) flour, plus extra for dusting
60 g (2 oz) white chocolate, finely chopped
80 g (3 oz) shop-bought pistachio cream (see *Intro*)
2 medium eggs
30 g (1 oz/ 2 tablespoons) caster (superfine) sugar

- TO DECORATE -

icing (confectioners') sugar, for dusting
2 tablespoons chopped pistachio

Preheat the oven to 180°C fan (400°F) and grease and flour four 6 cm (2½ in) diameter moulds.

Place the chocolate, butter and pistachio cream in a heatproof bowl and melt together in the microwave on high in three to four 20-second bursts, stirring between each one. Set aside to cool.

In a separate bowl and using a hand mixer, whisk the eggs with the caster sugar for about 4–5 minutes, or until super-fluffy, then add your melted pistachio mixture and mix everything together for a further minute. Finally, sift in the flour and stir once more until you have a smooth batter.

Divide the mixture between the prepared moulds and place on a baking tray. Bake for 17 minutes, then remove from the oven and allow the pistachio lava cakes to rest for 1 minute.

Flip each cake on to a small plate and sprinkle over icing sugar and chopped pistachios to decorate. Serve immediately.

APERITIVO

APERITIVO

APERITIVO

APERITIVO

APERITIVO

Aperitivo is a way of living in Italy. It is a moment before lunch or dinner when we gather for a drink and have a chat with our friends. At the bars in Italy, drinks are always served with some nibbles, from simple crisps and peanuts to pizzas, focaccias and even charcuterie boards or small pasta dishes – and the food is always free. Sometimes, they serve us so much food that it ends up becoming dinner, and we call this *apericena* (a word that comes from *aperitivo* and *cena*, which means 'dinner' in Italian).

In this chapter, I deliberately didn't include the well-known classic Italian drinks, as I thought you might know them already. Instead, I wanted to show you some of my favourite modern Italian cocktails, which you can use to impress your friends and family! Here, you will find some drinks that are perfect for *aperitivo*, but also some that are best served after a meal. My favourites? Lemon Sgroppino and Tiramisù Espresso Martini (pages 161 and 167) – *cin cin!*

MAMMA *Mia!*

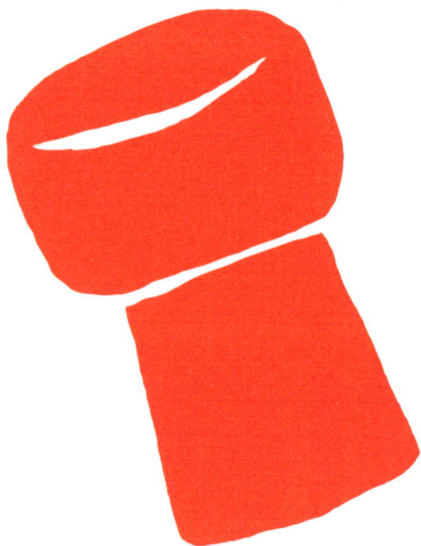

SUPER *Sexy!*

LEMON SGROPPINO

- SERVES -
4

- PREP TIME -
3 minutes

Sgroppino is a classic Italian summer cocktail, perfect for a drinking at the beach. It is usually served in Italian restaurants at the end of a meal to help with digestion. All you need are the ingredients and a blender.

100 g (3½ oz) lemon gelato
(shop-bought)
200 ml (7 fl oz/ scant
1 cup) prosecco
80 ml (2¾ fl oz/ ⅓ cup) vodka
lemon slices, to serve

Add all the ingredients to a blender, whizz together for a minute, then pour into four glasses. Serve very cold with a slice of lemon ... *Cin cin!*

- *Sexy Tip* -

Try making *sgroppino*
with strawberry or melon
ice cream instead!

FROZEN APEROL SPRITZ

- SERVES -
2

- PREP TIME -
5 minutes, plus freezing

I am sure you all know the Aperol spritz very well, but have you ever tried it frozen? Serve it really cold with some crisps and peanuts for your next *aperitivo ... mamma mia!*

200 ml (7 fl oz/ scant 1 cup) orange juice
1 small mango, peeled, stoned and chopped
90 ml (3 fl oz/ scant 1 cup) prosecco
20 ml (1½ tablespoons) soda water
60 ml (2 fl oz/ ¼ cup) Aperol
orange slices, to serve

Pour your orange juice into an ice cube tray, and place the chopped mango in a freezer-proof container. Freeze both for a couple of hours.

Once frozen, tip the orange ice cubes and frozen mango into a blender. Add the prosecco, soda water and Aperol, and blitz to combine. Pour into glasses and serve very cold, garnished with slices of fresh orange. *Cin cin!*

- Sexy Tip -

Instead of the mango, you can use an orange instead.

LIMONCELLO SPRITZ

Italians love a good spritz, and this limoncello version is the newest trend! If you have never had it, you have to try it immediately — it will become your new favourite drink!

ice cubes
90 ml (3 fl oz/ scant 1 cup) prosecco
60 ml (2 fl oz/ ¼ cup) limoncello
10 ml (2 teaspoons) lemon juice
30 ml (2 tablespoons) soda water
1 teaspoon lemon zest
1 sprig of mint

Fill a wine glass with ice, then add the prosecco, limoncello, lemon juice and soda water. Give it a nice stir with a spoon, and garnish with the lemon zest and sprig of mint. *Cin cin!*

TIRAMISÙ ESPRESSO MARTINI

- SERVES -
2

- PREP TIME -
10 minutes

If you like espresso martinis and you love tiramisù, this is the perfect recipe for you. Serve it at the end of a dinner party instead of the usual cup of coffee to surprise your guests!

80 ml (2¾ fl oz/ ⅓ cup) vodka
60 ml (2 fl oz/ ¼ cup) coffee liqueur
60 ml (2 fl oz/ ¼ cup) freshly brewed espresso
ice cubes
unsweetened cocoa powder, for dusting
6 coffee beans

- FOR THE TIRAMISU TOPPING -

100 ml (3½ fl oz/ scant ½ cup) double (heavy) cream
1 egg yolk
1½ tablespoons caster (superfine) sugar
100 g (3½ oz) mascarpone

First prepare the tiramisù topping. In a large bowl and with a hand mixer, whip the double cream for 90 seconds or until fluffy. In another bowl, combine the egg yolk and the sugar and, with a hand mixer, whisk together for 1 minute, or until the mixture becomes light and fluffy. Stir in the mascarpone cheese, and finally fold in the whipped cream. The tiramisù topping should not be too thick.

Now prepare the espresso martinis. Pour the vodka, coffee liqueur and freshly brewed espresso into a cocktail shaker. Add a couple of ice cubes, then close the lid and shake for about 1 minute.

Divide between two martini glasses, then spoon on the tiramisù topping. Serve dusted with cocoa powder and topped with coffee beans. *Cin cin!*

CHOCOLATE NEGRONI

- SERVES -
1

- PREP TIME -
5 minutes, plus chilling

Chocolate and orange make one of my favourite flavour combinations ever, and this chocolate negroni is an absolute dream! However, if you don't fancy this combination, don't worry. Just leave out the chocolate hazelnut cream to enjoy a classic negroni.

ice cubes
30 ml (2 tablespoons) gin
30 ml (2 tablespoons) Campari
30 ml (2 tablespoons) vermouth
2 tablespoons Chocolate
Hazelnut Cream (page 135)
orange slice, to serve

Place a glass in the refrigerator and leave to chill for 20 minutes.

Once chilled, add some ice cubes to the glass, then pour in the gin, Campari and vermouth, and stir with a spoon.

Spread the chocolate hazelnut cream around the rim of the glass, and serve with an orange slice on top. *Cin cin!*

ABOUT THE AUTHOR

Angelo Coassin is a passionate Italian cook who learned everything from his mamma and nonna. In 2020, he launched his Instagram and TikTok channels, **@cookingwithbello**, dedicated to creating fun and delicious Italian recipes. Since then he has amassed 1.4m Instagram followers and 1.7 million on TikTok.

ACKNOWLEDGEMENTS

Grazie to my followers! You encouraged me to pursue my journey as a creator.

Grazie to my mum Janet, my dad Carlo and my brother Francesco who have taught me what unconditional love is.

To my agents at Yellow Poppy Media, Anna, Geraldine and Kate, for always believing in my vision and my (sometimes) unconventional ideas.

To Hardie Grant. To my super sexy photographer Luke, my food stylist queens, Esther, El and Caitlin, and prop stylist Louie. To George Saad Studio for making this book so beautiful.

To my agents at Zenzero Talent Agency, my managers and all the brands who continue to support my work.

To Johanna for being the first to believe in me when I moved to London and to Alina and Johan!

To my big, beautiful Italian family: my great aunt Rosanna, my *nonni*, Luciano and Silvio, and my *nonne*, Silvana and Angelina. To all of my aunties, uncles and cousins: I want to thank every one of you for always making me feel loved. To my aunt Mara for the endless tiramisù, love and laughter. We miss you every day.

To Chips (aka John), one of the purest souls that I have ever encountered in my life. To your family Helen, Steve, Nick and Jonesy for making me feel at home.

To all my friends. I'm not going to list everyone but I HAVE TO mention Serxhio and Valeria. To Sara for washing my dishes, Llenia, my very first social media manager, Anna for editing my first profile picture and Tommy for (unconsciously) choosing the name 'Cooking with Bello'.

INDEX

Published in 2024 by Hardie Grant Books
(London)

Hardie Grant Books (London)
5th & 6th Floors
52–54 Southwark Street
London SE1 1UN

hardiegrantbooks.com

British Library Cataloguing-in-Publication
Data. A catalogue record for this book is
available from the British Library.

Cook Like a Real Italian
ISBN: 978-178488-7445

10 9 8 7 6 5 4 3 2 1

Publishing Director: Kajal Mistry
Senior Commissioning Editor: Kate Burkett
Photographer: Luke J Albert
Food Stylist: Esther Clark
Food Stylist Assistants: El Kemp and
Caitlin MacDonald
Prop Stylist: Louie Waller
Copy Editor: Tara O'Sullivan
Proofreader: Kathy Steer
Indexer: Cathy Heath
Design and illustrations: George Saad Studio
Senior Production Controller: Sabeena Atchia

Colour reproduction by p2d
Printed in China by C&C Offset Printing Co., Ltd.

FSC
MIX
Paper | Supporting
responsible forestry
FSC® C018179
www.fsc.org

SUPER
Sexy!